# Zapcrafts

# Zapcrafts

**Microwaves Are For Much More
Than Cooking**

## Nancy Birnes

**TEN SPEED PRESS**
Berkeley, California

1☉

**TEN SPEED PRESS**
P.O. Box 7123
Berkeley, California 94707

*Cover design by Fifth Street Design*
*Text design by Nancy Birnes*

**Library of Congress Cataloguing-in-Publication Data**

Birnes, Nancy.
    Zapcrafts : microwaves are for much more than cooking / by Nancy Birnes.
        p.        cm.
    ISBN   0-89815-290-9
    1. Handicraft.    2. Microwave cookery.        I. Title.
TT157.B54    1990
    745.5--dc20                                                    90-10784
                                                                          CIP

Printed in the United States of America

1  2  3  4  5  6  –  95  94  93  92  91  90

# Introduction

Anyone who has ever cooked with a microwave oven can attest to the appliance's versatility and ease. The more ideas people have for using microwave ovens the handier the microwave becomes. In Zapcrafts, I'm going to share with you the ways I've adapted my microwave oven for a busy lifestyle and for making health, beauty, and gift items for my family and friends. First, a note about different kinds of microwaves, wattages, and the different levels of power you'll be using.

For our purposes, I've based all of the recipes on a 600- to 700-watt oven. That's generally considered to be the standard in an industry where there are very few real standards. If you have an oven with a 500 watt output, add about 15 seconds of cooking time for the recipes. If you have an oven with a 400 watt output, you should add 30 seconds to the recipe instructions in the book.

Next are the power settings. By "High," I mean a full 100% of the microwave's power, "Medium High" means 75% power, "Medium" is 50%, "Medium Low" is about one third, and "Low" is about 25%. You will learn by trial and error how your own oven fares against this scale and will adjust your recipes and cooking times accordingly.

When the recipe calls for a glass container, you should use only heat-tempered glass. This is a specially designed material for use in high temperatures. Any glass that's not heat-tempered may be shattered by the heat of the food. That's one of the dangers of a microwave oven. You can't see any flames, but the food inside the containers gets hotter than it might over an open fire. Therefore, use only the utensils, bowls, and containers that are recommended for microwave use. Materials not recommended for your microwave can be dangerous. The same warning goes for plastic containers. Plastic that is not specifically recommended for microwave use should be avoided. The heat from food can melt the plastic and contaminate the food. Regular plastic containers should be used only for light reheating. Anything more will melt them.

Metal should not be used for primary cooking because the metal will reflect microwaves back to the oven itself. When the microwaves hit metal that is separated by air—as in a crumpled piece of aluminium foil—the energy becomes visible as a spark. This is known as "arcing," and it's what can happen if you have pieces of foil in your oven as you energize food. You can smooth out a piece of foil over the top of a container, if you are cooking vegetables in a small amount of water. The foil will prevent the microwaves from entering the container from the top while the ceramic or glass dish will allow them to enter from the bottom. As a result, the water will boil and the vegetables will steam without drying out.

Many of the recipes ask you to rotate your items midway through the cooking process. Rotation prevents items from becoming overcooked on one side and undercooked on another. Many of the newer microwaves have rotating cooking patterns or rotating trays which obviate the need for rotating the item itself. Unless your instruction book specifically tells you that you have a rotation pattern or unless your oven rotates the food on a spinning tray, assume that you will have to rotate the item during the cooking process.

Always let your items cool in the oven before you attempt to remove them. Many people are surprised to learn that items keep on cooking even after the power to the oven is turned off. Letting items sit for a minute or so allows the cooking process to stop and the item to cool. Putting your hands directly on an item to remove it from the oven before it has cooled can result in a burn if you aren't aware of this. I especially caution you against taking hot towels and washcloths directly from the oven and applying them to your face. You can get a nasty scalding. Even after they've been allowed to cool off a bit, hot towels are still plenty hot and will do the job you want. If they're not hot enough, you can always reheat. Better to err on the side of caution than risk a burn.

Finally, a word about sterilization and bacteria. You'll be using many of the recipes in this book for health and beauty purposes. This means that when you store items, you should store them in clean or sterilized containers. If you are saving containers for reuse, make sure that after you've washed and dried them you store them with the lids off. Leaving lids on may allow bacteria cultures to grow in the dampness. By storing your containers with the lids off and making sure they're clean before you use them, you help prevent bacterial infections. This becomes especially important when you prepare skin care recipes or items for the bath.

Feel free to experiment. Many of the recipes in this book are the results of experimenting with an idea, a spice, a fragrance, or a taste. Create, indulge your fantasies, let your imagination be your guide. If you follow simple safety rules and err on the side of caution, you can have loads of fun and save money at the same time.

Enjoy!

# Contents

# 1

# BEAUTY IN A FLASH

*The following preparations will show you how a warm, fresh, homemade facial product can be customized for your own ever-changing skin type. These recipes will work quicker and penetrate deeper than any cold, impersonal, off-the-shelf product. They are made from herbs and flowers that can be dried in the microwave oven and then steeped and bubbled into magical creams and lotions. All the items in this chapter are safe, very effective, and even fun to make. In addition, they can save you hundreds of dollars over the same items from department and drugstores because not one extra penny is spent on packaging or advertising. Here is everything you need to pamper yourself, your baby, your best friend, and your wallet.*

# *Recipes and Instructions*

# Forever Young Facial Cream

*This basic recipe can be modified for oily skin, dry skin, skin that's aging too quickly, or skin that needs vitamin E to stay supple and healthy. It's a versatile formula and I've found it to be a true anti-aging secret. It's a valuable part of anyone's spa routine at home.*

**2 tablespoons glycerin**
**2 tablespoons cocoa butter**
**1/2 cup safflower or sesame oil**
**1 cup Aquavita or rosewater**
**1/8 teaspoon oil of violet or similar essential oil**

1   Melt glycerin and cocoa butter together in a glass bowl and microwave on medium power for 3 minutes. Remove.

2   Beat in oil slowly, add Aquavita or rosewater and heat on medium power for 2 minutes, stir, and continue for 2 minutes.

3   Add oil of violet or other essential oil, stir completely, and let cool while stiring constantly.

4   Pour mixture into a jar and shake until it is completely mixed and cool.

### How to Use:
*Apply moisturizing lotion after rinsing as the final touch to your facial cleansing, or apply lightly for nighttime moisturizing. You can also apply this mixture lavishly and gently pat off for use as a cleansing cream.*

### Variations:

For a moisturizing vitamin E cream, add 1/4 cup wheat germ oil to your formula and massage in lightly before bedtime. After one month's nightly regimen, you should notice a real difference in the way your skin looks.

For a skin softener, add 1/4 cup skim milk or 2 tablespoons powdered milk and melt 1 tablespoon of honey into the oil mixture. Apply first thing in the morning, then rinse and apply makeup. You can also use the milk and honey cream as a nighttime moisturizer or as a complement to your vitamin E cream.

For a mildly abrasive cleansing cream as well as a skin restorative, add 1 tablespoon chopped fresh mint and 1/4 cup thoroughly mashed avocado to your basic lotion mixture. This green formula will act like a magic elixir to clean and remove grease and oil while keeping skin moist and young.

For a dry skin cream, in additon to the rosewater in the basic recipe, add 1/2 ounce beeswax and 1 tablespoon virgin olive oil (preferably a first pressing), and apply lightly as needed. If you feel your skin still needs more moisture, apply the cream in heavier amounts.

**Yield:**   14 ounces

# Bright Skin Bleaching Cream

*Scarlett O'Hara might have used this simple cream to tone down her freckles and to give her skin a pale, translucent quality. If you can't or won't tan in the summer, try making your skin as bright as possible with this preparation.*

*Your microwave oven on low power will gently warm the oils and waters and melt the waxes for your cream. Stir vigorously when mixing the oils, waxes, and liquids—your cream will thicken as it cools.*

*Don't worry about finding the ingredients: they are usually at hand. The mineral oil is in every supermarket in the medicine section and you can always find whey at the top of your yogurt—it's the thin watery substance. Just pour it off and use it in this recipe.*

**1/4 cup mineral oil
1 tablespoon beeswax or paraffin
1/4 cup lemon juice
1/2 cup whey**

1   Melt the paraffin and mineral oil in the microwave in separate bowls on low/medium power for 90 seconds. Watch carefully, because wax and oil can splatter in your oven if they are left unattended. When the wax is nearly melted, remove both bowls and set aside while you microwave the lemon juice and whey on the lowest setting for 2 minutes.

2   Pour the melted wax into a glass bowl and gradually stir in the warm oil, mixing constantly and vigorously. Keep mixing and add the warm lemon juice and whey. Cover and refrigerate for 2 hours or until cream is set.

3   Remove the mixture from the refrigerator and whip with an electric hand mixer or with a wire whisk until light and creamy. You may add a drop of your favorite perfume at this step, if desired.

4   Store cream in the refrigerator during the summer months and use up within 4 to 6 weeks.

*Yield:*  8 ounces

# Skin-tightening Masks

*In the event that you have neither the time nor the inclination to make your own cream, and especially if you find yourself suddenly out of whey, here are two masks that will lighten and tighten your skin.*

## Lemon Lightening Pack

**2 tablespoons fuller's earth**
**1 teaspoon lemon juice**
**1 teaspoon buttermilk**

Mix all ingredients into a paste and microwave on low power for 90 seconds to blend it further. Let cool before you use it. Then apply to the skin in light upward strokes. Sit back with your feet up for 20 minutes; rinse with the **Skin Bleaching Tonic**, following.

## Skin Bleaching Tonic

**1 lemon, sliced**
**1 cup white wine**
**1 tablespoon sugar**

1   Place lemon slices and wine in a glass bowl and bring to a boil in microwave on high power for 2 minutes and then continue on medium for 90 seconds. Remove from the heat, stir in the sugar, and let cool.

2   Strain the mixture and store in a tightly capped bottle. Use as a skin refresher and after using the **Lemon Lightening Pack**.

*Yield:*   1 treatment

# Fresh Facial Creams

*These creams are soothing for simple cases of windburn, sunburn, insect bites, or poison ivy, and they can even calm the ravages of air pollution if you apply some right after cleansing your face. As with the creation of any creams, remember the cooking lessons learned from making simple mayonnaise—slowly, very slowly, add the oil—drop by drop—to the wax. Don't rush this step and you will be rewarded with smooth, silky cream.*

## Anti-aging Cream

*If you smooth a bit of this antiwrinkle preparation every night around the tender skin of your face and neck, and remember to smile every time you think about aging, I promise you will never have to worry about lines and wrinkles. It's not that you won't have them—it's just that you won't worry about them so much.*

**1 ounce glycerin**
**1 ounce witch hazel**
**1/2 ounce rosewater**
**3 tablespoons honey**
**3 tablespoons wheat germ oil**

1   Combine the first four ingredients in a glass bowl and gradually beat in the wheat germ oil. Blend in the microwave on low power for 90 seconds, cool, and gently whisk until they are thoroughly combined.

2   Store the emulsion in a tightly sealed container at room temperature. It should last for at least 1 month, which is about when you will want to make up a new batch.

### How to Use:

*Massage the solution into the skin around your eyes and mouth, using a circular and upward motion. This motion will counteract the natural droop of gravity. If you have the time, it's a good idea to hang your head over the edge of the bed and massage the cream in while you're partially upside down. This seems to bring a nice blush to the skin as well.*

**Yield:**  5 1/2 ounces

# Soothing Cucumber Cream

**1 whole cucumber, unpeeled**
**1/2 ounce white paraffin**
**2 ounces sweet almond oil**

1   Cut the cucumber into chunks and puree it in the food processor or blender. Strain the pulp through a strainer lined with cheesecloth. Discard the peel and seeds.

2   Melt the wax in the microwave on medium or medium/ low power for 90 seconds, making sure that the wax does not splatter. As soon as the wax is melted, remove from the oven and slowly add the oil, stirring gently. Add strained cucumber and blend thoroughly.

3   Remove and cover with a clean kitchen towel. Let the mixture cool very slowly to prevent crystals from forming in the wax. Stir mixture once or twice until cool.

4   When the mixture is completely cool and smooth, store it in a labeled, tightly capped glass container in the refrigerator. Cream will keep for 60 days.

**Yield:**  4 ounces

# Chamomile Mask

*Chamomile leaves were once thought by the ancients to have magical restorative powers. They used chamomile in everything—from tea to liniment to shampoo—to ward off infection, thin the blood, thicken the blood, and stimulate the digestive system.*

*Chamomile was also used in bandages and dressings in time of war because it was said to be able to prevent gangrene and infection of wounds. Needless to say, this mask might just be able to do something good for you, no matter what ails your skin.*

**1/2 cup dried chamomile
2 tablespoons honey
2 tablespoons oatmeal (optional)**

1   Microwave chamomile in just enough water to cover on high power for 4 minutes and on medium power for 6 minutes. When reduced by about a third, add honey and continue to microwave on medium power for 3 minutes.

2   Add oatmeal, if desired, for a little more abrasiveness, and let mixture cool. Use mixture at room temperature or just slightly warmed.

**How to Use:**
*Apply in an upward circular motion to smooth out wrinkles and tighten skin. Let mask remain for 45 minutes to 1 hour. Peel off and rinse with warm water.*

**Yield:** 1 treatment

# Cucumber-Mint Mask

*This mask is designed to be tangy—an early morning pick-me-up for those Mondays when you want to start off the week with a little extra confidence or pizzazz. If you're allowing yourself a pampering day on Sunday, this Monday morning finale puts a fine finish on the entire weekend.*

*There are two variations of the cucumber-mint mask which you may want to consider: if you mix oatmeal into the basic recipe, you will have a facial scrub that is moderately abrasive and thoroughly cleansing. If you mix yogurt into the recipe, you will have a soothing mask that controls skin bacteria.*

**1/2 cup cucumber solids**
**2 tablespoons mint extract**
*or*
**1/4 cup fresh mint leaves, chopped**
**1 tablespoon peppermint extract (optional)**
**2 cups water**

1   Microwave cucumber solids and water on high power for 4 minutes. Combine mint extract or chopped mint leaves with peppermint (if using) and add to cucumber mixture. Continue microwaving on medium power for 5 minutes. Remove and let stand for 15 minutes. Use when cool to the touch.

2   Store any excess in refrigerator until ready for use. Mixture will keep for up to 30 days in a sterilized glass jar with a tight-fitting lid.

### How to Use:

Warm a portion of the mixture in the microwave for 2 minutes on low to medium power. Apply to a clean face, let it remain on your skin for 30 minutes, and remove by washing gently with warm water and a mild soap.

### Variations:

Add a handful (about 1/2 cup) of raw oatmeal or rolled oats to the warmed cucumber mixture to make a mild to moderately abrasive cleanser. Abrasive cleansers peel off the top layers of skin cells, so proceed carefully. If this is the mask you want, work the mixture in with your fingertips. Let it dry thoroughly and slough off the excess oatmeal with a soft, dry terry towel. Wash with warm water and a mild soap and finish off with one of the astringent rinses on page 14 or 18.

You can also add 1 to 3 tablespoons plain yogurt (with active cultures) which will help to kill skin viruses or fungus inflammations. However, these preparations are not antibiotic and will not replace either medical advice or a doctor's prescription. Used on a regular basis, a yogurt-based mask is a good preventive measure for healthy skin. Use no more than 3 tablespoons of yogurt in the mixture at a time.

**Yield:**   18 ounces

# Yogurt-Milk Mask

*Here's how you can use the cucumber pulp left over from your shaving and skin lotions (see pages 11 and 26). Just boil the cucumber solids, let them cool, mix with yogurt, apply, sit back, and let the years peel away. The combination of vitamin C–rich cucumber and yogurt cultures not only cleanses, it also counteracts skin bacteria.*

**1/2 cup cucumber solids**
**2 cups water**
**1/2 cup fresh lemon juice**
**4 tablespoons active yogurt culture (plain yogurt)**
**1 cup skim milk**

1   Microwave the cucumber solids in the water on high power for 4 minutes. Add lemon juice and microwave on medium power for 4 minutes or until mixture is reduced by about half. Remove and let cool.

2   Mix yogurt and skim milk in a blender on low power, add to cucumber pulp, and store in a sterilized container in the refrigerator. Mixture will keep for 30 days.

### How to Use:

*Heat a small portion (about 1/4 cup) by microwaving on low power for a maximum of 90 seconds. Mask should not be hot. Do not overheat or you will destroy the yogurt culture.*

*Apply facial mask liberally to areas under eyes, on cheeks, around nose, and under chin. Let mask remain on your face for 30 minutes, peel off, and finish with a vinegar or herbal rinse, page 18 or 19.*

**Yield:**   16 ounces

# Aqua de Granatum

*Aqua de Granatum, or pomegranate lotion, is a recipe that goes back to the ancient Macedonians, who gave it to the Romans. It is said that Alexander the Great's legions brought it back from from Persia, where they had discovered that highborn Persian women used it as a beauty treatment and as a way to tighten the skin around their breasts and thighs.*

*This treatment became a fad during the reign of Pompey and again under Justinian, who banned using the fruit as a cosmetic because he considered it a pagan practice. Rumor has it that the use of pomegranate lotion still continues among high-ranking women in the Persian crescent even though its use has been suppressed in recent years.*

**1 pomegranate**
**1/2 cup white vinegar**
**4 cups water**

Peel the pomegranate. (Keep the seeds for eating or for a salad.) Dissolve the peel in a mixture of water and vinegar by boiling it in your microwave on high power for 4 minutes and simmering it on low/medium power for 10 to 15 minutes or until the peel is completely dissolved. Strain and store in a sterilized jar in the refrigerator.

***How to Use:***
*The liquid can be used cold or heated. It makes an excellent astringent or skin cleanser.*

***Yield:***  36 ounces

# Green Facial Mask

*Any facial mask prepared with green vegetables restores skin clarity in two ways: Green vegetables remove skin oils and grease and they are a primary source of iron and vitamin B, two nutrients often lacking in the diet but necessary for healthy skin. This mask is particularly healthy for teenagers, especially those who neglect green vegetables in their diets.*

**1 cup spinach, kale, collards,**
*or*
**Other green leafy vegetable**
**1/2 cup parsley**
**1 cup carrot leaves**
**4 cups water**

1   Chop all the greens as finely as possible or process in a food processor until greens form a thick paste.

2   Mix the chopped greens or the paste with the water and microwave on high power for 4 minutes, then reduce to medium/low power and cook for 10 minutes or until the solids are completely dissolved. Remove from oven, strain, and let cool before using. Store in refrigerator in a tightly capped, sterilized glass jar.

### How to Use:
*Apply mask at room temperature in upward sweeping motions to smooth out skin. Let dry for 45 minutes, peel off, and rinse face with warm water. Wash with a mild soap and finish off with an astringent facial rinse, page 14 or 18, if desired.*

**Yield:**   34 ounces

# Skin Scrubbing Grains and Creams

*Scrubs are different from masks in that you are expected to take an active part in their application and gently agitate the materials on your skin to create a sloughing action. Only use these scrubs on skin that can take it—firm, young, oily, or resilient skin.*

## Oatmeal-Citrus Scrubbing Grains

**1 cup dried orange and lemon peel**
**1 cup uncooked oatmeal**
**1 cup almonds**

1    Dry peels in the microwave by placing them in a shallow tray and cooking at low to medium power for 5 minutes. Rotate the tray and check for dryness. Dry peels completely.

2    Combine peels, oatmeal, and almonds in a bowl and cook in microwave on low power for 90 seconds. Place mixture in a blender or food processor and whirl until the mixture is a fine powder. Store powder in an attractive container near the bathroom sink and use a tiny portion as needed.

***How to Use:***
*Place a tiny bit of the scrub in the palm of your hand and moisten with a few drops of warm tap water. Rub the paste onto your face with a gentle circular and upward motion. Rinse off with tepid water and pat dry. Finish your cleansing by rinsing your face with **Facial Rinsing Lotion**, page 18, or smoothing on some of the **Fresh Facial Cream**, page 8.*

***Idea:***
*Store this scrub in one of the big shakers meant for the kitchen and keep it handy at the bathroom sink.*

***Yield:*** 24 ounces

# Oatmeal-Honey Scrubbing Cream

*Because this mixture is cooked for a minute or so in the microwave before you use it, the resulting scrub is much more gentle than one with raw oatmeal. Thus, even the most fragile complexion can still benefit from a little sloughing off.*

**1/2 cup uncooked oatmeal**
**1 tablespoon honey**
**1 tablespoon cider vinegar**
**1 teaspoon almonds, ground**

Combine all ingredients in a glass bowl and blend in microwave on low for 90 seconds. Remove and let cool slightly before using.

***How to Use:***
*First steam your face with one of the **Herbal Steam Facials**, pages 20 and 21, or wet a clean washcloth with warm water and lay it on your face for a minute. Apply the oatmeal mixture to your face, being careful to avoid the sensitive area around your eyes. Let mixture dry on your skin.*

*Gently rub the dried mixture off with a clean terry washcloth or towel. Lean over the sink and rub your face in brisk but gentle circles with the cloth. Rinse with warm water, pat dry, and apply one of the **Fresh Facial Creams** described in this chapter.*

***Yield:*** 5 1/2 ounces

# Facial Rinsing Lotions

*These facial lotions soothe and seem to revitalize oily skin. Because they are each so refreshing, either one is ideal after a sauna or long session in the sun. If you cannot find chamomile blossoms at your health food store or pharmacy, try substituting some sprigs of fresh lilac, wisteria, heather, or magnolia blossoms instead.*

## Rosemary Chamomile Rinse

**1 tablespoon dried rosemary**
***or***
**2 tablespoons fresh rosemary**
**2 tablespoons dried chamomile**
***or***
**1/4 cup fresh chamomile flowers**
**4 cups water**

1   If using fresh herbs, dry them in the microwave on medium/low power for 3-minute cycles until dry. Store the dried materials in a sterilized glass jar until you use them.

2   Combine herbs and water in a glass bowl and microwave on high power for 3 minutes, reduce to medium, and microwave for 3 minutes more. Cool, strain, and retain the liquid. Cool before using.

***How to Use:***
   *Wipe the liquid over your face with a fresh cotton square or pour it into a pump-type plastic or glass container and spritz it on your face. Let the solution remain for 30 minutes, rinse with cool water, and then pat dry.*

*Tip:*

It's never a bad idea to apply the facial, close the curtains, and relax with your feet elevated higher than your head for 20 or 30 minutes.

Try brewing a big mug of tea with 2 teabags, squeeze out the teabags as usual, let them cool slightly, and then apply them to your closed eyes while you rest. The tannin in the tea is said to reduce puffiness around your eyes.

*Yield:* 32 ounces

# Cider Stabilizing Rinse

The natural acidic composition of the vinegar will restore and stabilize the acid balance that is necessary to protect your skin from blemishes and infection. Use this rinse immediately after washing for the most benefit.

**1/4 cup cider vinegar**
**1/4 cup water**

Combine vinegar and water, microwave on low power for 90 seconds, cool thoroughly before using. Gently wipe your face with the mixture. Let this rinse dry on your skin.

*Yield:* 4 ounces

# Herbal Steam Facial

*There is no better way to open clogged pores for a deep-down cleaning than to use an old-fashioned steam tent. This method has been used in spas around the world to give facial skin an inner glow of health and cleanliness. It's safe to say that that's why the rich always look so rich: they've been cleaned from the inside out. Now you can look as rich as the Gstaad and Aspen crowd because you'll be using the same steam-cleaning methods they do.*

**2 tablespoons dried fennel seed**
**2 tablespoons dried chamomile**
**2 tablespoons dried licorice root**
**2 tablespoons dried anise**
**2 tablespoons dried lavender**
**4 cups mineral water**
**1 tablespoon wheat germ oil**

1   Combine herbs and microwave together on low power for 90 seconds.

2   Microwave water and wheat germ oil in a glass bowl on high power for 5 minutes or until boiling briskly. Add herb mixture.

3   Simmer for 2 minutes on medium power. Remove and store extra rinse in a sterilized jar with a tightly fitting lid. Mixture will keep in the refrigerator for up to 30 days.

### *How to Use:*
*Tie back your hair or wear a shower cap and drape a large towel completely over your head and the bowl to form a tent. Keep your face 8 inches from the steaming water and let*

*the steam fill the towel tent for about 10 minutes. Rinse your face with cold water and a vinegar-based rinse, page 19, as an astringent to close pores.*

### *Variations:*

*To stimulate skin, add a handful of nettles, rosemary, thyme, or tarragon.*

*To fight skin eruptions, use double the amounts of licorice and anise.*

*For oily skin, add lemon peel and birch bark to herbs.*

*To tighten wrinkled skin, add mint extract, mint leaves, or peppermint leaves to herbal mixture.*

*For a refreshing vitamin C orange mist, add orange peel, orange extract, or orange leaves to herbal mixture.*

*As a preshave facial and heavy beard softener, add extra lavender and anise to your herbal mixture with just a touch of musk oil.*

**Yield:**   32 ounces

# Fountain of Youth Facial Rinse

*Here is a basic facial rinse and conditioner that you can modify with different herbs, fruits, flowers, and spices. The ingredients can be either fresh or dried. You can use it after applying a facial mask, before bedtime, or when you first wake up as part of a morning regimen. Men can also use this before or after shaving, especially if they add bay leaves or other spices to the mix.*

**1 tablespoon sage**
**1 tablespoon rosemary**
**1 tablespoon rose petals**
**1 tablespoon strawberry leaves**
**1 cup strawberries**
**2 cups vinegar**
**1 cup apple cider**
**1 cup rosewater**

1   Combine all herbs, petals, and leaves and any additional spices (see above) and microwave on low power for 2 minutes.

2   Mix berries, vinegar, cider, and rosewater and microwave on medium power for 3 minutes. Remove and while solution is still hot pour over dried leaf mixture. Let stand for 1 hour.

3   Microwave on low power for 30 minutes, let cool. Pour mixture into a large sterilized glass jar with a tightly fitting lid. Let stand for 1 week at room temperature to cure.

4   Strain and store in a sterilized container. You can also divide the facial rinse into smaller portions for a travel kit.

### How to Use:

Use as a rinse after a facial or as an aftershave, or you can use this solution as an afterbath splash or as a splash after your friction rubdown. Rinse also works as a pick-me-up if you are on long drives or long business flights when you don't have time to freshen up between aircraft changes.

You can freshen up anywhere with a quick application of your herbal-spice facial rinse. The vinegar and rosewater have an additional astringent function which tightens skin and closes pores. That's what makes it ideal as an aftershave as well as a cleansing rinse.

### Variations:

This rinse is nothing if not versatile. Use any of your favorite berries or favorite spices, and the basic recipe remains the same. Try huckleberries, raspberries, or tart limes for variety. It's like having a personal parfumier in your own microwave.

**Yield:**   32 ounces

# Aftershave Facesavers

*Nothing is harder on a man's face than shaving or a shake-out in the junk-bond market. There's nothing you can do about the junk-bond market, but there's a lot you can do about shaving. Shaving removes the vital acids from the skin and this preparation will restore the skin's acid balance to a proper level after washing away the shaving suds. Splash it on with abandon, and it will also heal tiny nicks and razor chinks, giving your skin a healthy glow in the bargain.*

*I've included a few different scents for different moods and different formulas for different types of skin—try each and see which one your skin likes best.*

## Young Man's Citrus Splash

*This recipe is fine for oily or problem skin, but it may be too drying for an older and more wizened face. If you like the mixture but would like it to be less drying, reduce the isopropyl alcohol to 1 tablespoon.*

**1 cucumber**
**1 teaspoon dried mint or 2 sprigs fresh mint**
**1 cup witch hazel**
**1/4 cup isopropyl alcohol**
**1/4 cup lemon juice**
**1/4 cup lime juice**

1   Chop cucumber and place it, peel and all, in the blender. Blend on high power for 1 to 2 minutes. Strain the pulp through a cheesecloth-lined sieve or through a coffee filter, retaining the pulp for **Cucumber-Mint Mask**, page 11.

2   Crush the mint between two spoons to bruise it and combine it with the cucumber juice and other liquids. Microwave

the mixture on low/medium power for 1 minute, then let sit and cool for 30 minutes.

3   Strain and store in a tightly capped bottle or plastic pump-type atomizer. Keep the aftershave in the refrigerator in the hottest months for an extra refreshing splash.

**Variations:**
    *Try replacing the isopropyl alcohol with an equal quantity of vodka for a different blend. One tablespoon of glycerin will further soften the drying effect of this aftershave.*

**Yield:** 14 ounces

# Savory Herb Splash

*The herbs and spices listed here are one version of this splash to try, and then check under* **Variations** *for others that might suit your nose or your fancy. Or, each time you mix up a batch of aftershave, you might try a different combination.*

**1 tablespoon sage**
**1 tablespoon thyme**
**1 tablespoon savory**
**1 tablespoon ground cloves**
**1 tablespoon bay leaves, crumbled**
**2 cups white vinegar**
**1/4 cup honey**

1   If you use fresh herbs, you should use about 1/8 cup (or twice the amount) for each tablespoon of dry. Dry your herbs by microwaving on medium or low/medium power for 2-minute cycles, checking after each cycle.

2   After you've thoroughly dried the herbs, combine all ingredients, microwave on low power for 90 seconds to blend, let cool, and store in a sterilized glass jar for 1 week. Shake

occasionally to mix contents. Strain and pour into a sterilized, tightly capped bottle.

### *Variations:*

*Another time, try a tablespoon of coriander seeds or rosemary, and use apple cider vinegar.*

**Yield:**   16 ounces

# Cucumber Aftershave Splash

*Naturally kinder and gentler is better for any age skin, and this skin tonic is made from cucumbers to cool razor burn while adding soothing vitamin C to your skin routine.*

**1/2 whole cucumber**
**1/4 cup mint extract**
**1/2 cup water**

1   Blend cucumber, incuding rind, on the highest blender setting or in the food processor until the mixture is liquefied. Add mint extract and blend for another 30 seconds.

2   Strain and save solids for facial mask.

3   Add strained mixture to water and microwave on high power for 3 minutes and medium power for 2 minutes. Remove and let stand for 10 minutes before using.

4   Store in a sterilized container in the refrigerator.

### *How to Use:*

*Splash on face and neck after shaving or after showering or steam bath.*

**Yield:**   6 ounces

# Vitamin E Aftershave

*Here is a spa treatment that both men and women can enjoy—it's great not only after shaving but also after a steam bath or sauna, or on very wintry days when the cold winds freeze and abrade your skin.*

*The basis of this superior recipe is wheat germ oil, a wonderful source of vitamin E. You can buy it at your local health food store or even from an equestrian supply, farm, or cattle-feed dealer as a horse food supplement. If you purchase your wheat-germ oil from any place other than a food store, just remember to label it and restrict it to external, or topical, use.*

**1 cup wheat germ oil**
**1/4 cup witch hazel**
**2 tablespoons mint extract**
*or*
**5 sprigs fresh mint leaves, bruised**
**1/4 orange**
*or*
**1/2 lemon**
*or*
**1 lime**

1   Combine all ingredients in a blender on low power for 90 seconds, then high for 1 minute, or pour mixture into a glass jar with a tight-fitting lid and shake vigorously for 2 minutes.

2   Microwave mixture on medium/low power for 4 minutes. Remove. Strain and discard solids.

3   Simmer in microwave on low for 5 minutes more. Bottle the mixture in a sterilized glass jar or cruet with a tight-fitting lid. Store in refrigerator in warm weather. Mixture will remain fresh for about 2 months.

### How to Use:

Think of this potion as your old-age insurance in a bottle. Use only a tiny amount at a time and warm it in the microwave if you've stored the mix in the refrigerator.

Try it as a sauna treatment, pre- or post-shower or bath toner, or as a preshave hot-oil skin conditioner. Take a small portion out of the refrigerator, microwave on medium/low power for 1 minute and on low for 1 minute more. Wait until it is hot but not scalding and apply to skin. Let the oil remain on your skin for 10 or so minutes or more, especially if you're going into the dry heat of a sauna. Then shave or shower off.

As an aftershave, apply warm, not hot, oil to skin, cover face with a warm towel, and let it remain for about a minute. Then splash on white vinegar or one of the aftershave splashes on pages 24 and 26 to refine pores and tighten skin. If plain vinegar is too harsh, you can dilute it with water in equal parts or use 1 part vinegar to 2 or 3 parts water.

### Ideas:

As a spa treatment, hot-oil facials can be applied while you are soaking in your tub, resting sore muscles on a heating pad, or simply reading your morning newspaper and drinking a glass of fresh orange juice.

To get the full benefit of a hot-oil treatment, you might try this: hang your head over the edge of the bed and massage the oil into your face with a gentle circular motion while you're partially upside down. Close your eyes, think happy thoughts, and let the vitamin E do its work. You also reverse the wrinkle lines and turn sad expressions into happy ones. When you're finished soothing your skin, rise up very slowly to let the blood flow readjust itself, wait 2 or 3 minutes, and then get up to finish shaving or showering.

**Yield:**   11 ounces

# 2

# Spa Secrets in a Split Second

*The items in this chapter are for the full-body pampering of men, women, and children. You will enjoy preparing health and beauty supplies and using them to relax and baby yourself and your loved ones. You will also save hundreds of dollars in the process by creating your own personal "European" spa at home with simple ingredients and products that you warm in your microwave for a soothing treat as you prepare yourself for the pampering of a lifetime in your own kitchen-based health club. Your tired, aching body never had it so good.*

## *Recipes and Instructions*

# Healthy Secret Herbal Shampoo

*The real secret of herbs may never be unlocked, but this shampoo is gentle, infinitely variable, and will leave your hair soft and smelling wonderful. Don't expect mountains of soapy lather from this shampoo, however—its cleaning action is gentle and pervasive rather than supersudsy.*

*Try to use fresh herbs whenever possible because purchased herbs are very expensive. You can dry the herbs yourself for a fraction of the cost. Remember also that 2 tablespoons of dried herbs equal about 6 to 8 leaves (or sprigs) fresh. Don't worry if you don't have one or more of the herbs listed here. The shampoo works just as well with a wide variety of different herbs and spices, and you can vary it season by season, or customize it for your own hair color.*

**1 tablespoon dried or 5 sprigs fresh sage**
**1 tablespoon dried or 5 sprigs fresh rosemary**
**1 tablespoon dried or 5 sprigs fresh nettle**
**1 tablespoon dried or 5 leaves fresh peppermint**
**2 tablespoons dried or 8 sprigs fresh red clover**
**2 tablespoons dried or 8 sprigs fresh chamomile**
**1/4 cup orange peel**
**1/4 cup marigold flowers**
**1/4 cup birch buds and leaves**
**1 tablespoon dried orrisroot**
**5 cups water**
**2 tablespoons aloe gel**
**3/4 cup castile soap**
**Few drops of your favorite perfume or essential oil**

1   If using fresh herbs, dry them in the microwave on medium power for 2 minutes, checking for dryness and repeat-

ing the cycle if necessary. Stir the dried herbs together with the water in an enamel or glass bowl and microwave on high power for 3 minutes and then on medium for 4 to 5 minutes. Remove, cover, and let steep for 30 minutes. Strain the liquid and discard the herbs.

2   In a blender, combine 1 cup of the herb liquid with the aloe gel and blend on low speed until smooth.

3   In a glass or enamel bowl, blend the soap and the remaining liquid, then whip with a wire whisk until smooth and frothy. Add the blender liquid.

4   Pour the mixture into the containers of your choice and add the scent last, a few drops to each container. Shake to disperse the scent. Shampoo will keep for 1 to 2 months.

### Variations:

For blond hair, double the chamomile and omit the sage. For brunet hair, double the sage and omit the chamomile.

For oily hair, add 1/2 cup lemon peel. For dry hair, increase the marigold to 1/2 cup.

If the castile soap isn't bubbling enough for your taste, try mixing 1/2 cup of an inexpensive brand of unscented shampoo to 1/4 cup castile soap. Vary the proportions of the two until you get the sudsing action you like.

Try these two unusual ingredients for another shampoo, but keep the proportions of 3/4 cup castile soap to 5 cups liquid:

**2 teaspoons fresh birch juice**
**1/2 cup comfrey root**

**Yield:**   40 ounces

# Rinses and Toners for Your Hair

*These rinses will make your hair sparkle and they will also completely rinse out any residue from detergent-based shampoos or commercial conditioners. You can even customize the rinse for either light or dark hair.*

*Chamomile can be purchased from the pharmacy or the health food store. Sometimes it is sold in bulk in the form of tea, and it's smart to stock up on it because it's good for you, inside and out. It is extremely expensive at the pharmacy, where it is sold as a medicine in a little white container, so whenever possible, learn to identify the flower and pick and dry your own. Chamomile is a plentiful, common flower that grows wild all over the country in the late spring and summer, so you shouldn't have too much trouble gathering and drying your own blossoms.*

## Herbal Rinse for Normal Hair

*Use this rinse as a natural finish to **Healthy Secret Herbal Shampoo** (page 31). Just like the shampoo, this rinse can be customized to suit light, dark, dry, or oily hair. The important ingredient is the vinegar, which restores the natural acid balance of the hair and takes out any trace of soap.*

**1/2 cup white vinegar**
**1/2 cup water**
**2 tablespoons dried rosemary**
**2 tablespoons dried red clover buds**
**2 tablespoons dried nettle**

1    Combine all ingredients and microwave on high power for 3 minutes, until mixture is at rolling boil. Reduce to medium for 5 minutes and then remove from oven, cover, and let steep for 30 minutes.

2    Strain and pour into a glass or plastic container. Rinse will keep for 1 to 2 months.

**How to Use:**
   *After shampooing, pour 1/2 cup over hair; work through thoroughly and leave on hair for 2 minutes. Rinse.*

*Yield:* 8 ounces

# Lemon Rinse for Light Hair

**2 cups white vinegar**
**2 cups water**
**1/4 cup lemon juice**
**1/4 cup chamomile flowers**

Combine ingredients and microwave on high power for 3 minutes. Strain, discard flowers, or use them in your garden compost. Cool and store in a tightly capped bottle.

**How to Use:**
   *After shampooing, pour 1/2 cup over hair; work through thoroughly and leave on hair for 2 minutes. Rinse.*

*Yield:* 36 ounces

# Sage Rinse for Dark Hair

**2 cups malt or red wine vinegar**
**2 cups water**
**1/4 cup sage**

Combine ingredients amd microwave on high power for 3 minutes. Strain, cool, and store in a tightly capped bottle.

### How to Use:
*After shampooing, pour 1/2 cup over hair; work through thoroughly and leave on hair for 2 minutes. Rinse.*

**Yield:**  32 ounces

# Sea Rinse for Damaged Hair

**1/4 cup sea kelp**
**1 cup either Lemon or Sage Rinse**

Combine kelp and rinse in a pint- or quart-size jar, cap tightly, and shake well.

### How to Use:
*Apply generously to freshly shampooed hair, leave on for 20 minutes, and then rinse thoroughly.*

**Yield:**  8 ounces

# Dandruff Control Rinse

**1 cup apple cider vinegar**
**6 aspirins, crushed**
**1/4 cup witch hazel**

Combine all ingredients, microwave on medium power for 90 seconds, remove to cool, and store in a tightly capped jar or bottle.

### How to Use:
*After shampooing, gently massage rinse into your hair, leave it on for 10 minutes, and then rinse again with warm water.*

**Yield:**  10 ounces

# Dandruff Remover

*Here's an inexpensive and nifty way to remove dandruff flakes forever. You use dried rosemary in a solution with borax soap and sponge onto the scalp. In a few days, even your best friends will forget you ever had a dandruff problem.*

**2 tablespoons dried rosemary**
**1 cup water**
**1 tablespoon borax**

Steep rosemary in water by microwaving on high power for 3 minutes and then on medium for 4 minutes. Remove and add borax. Let stand to reach room temperature.

### How to Use:
*Each night, dab the solution onto the scalp in a circular motion that stimulates the scalp without pulling on the hair. Let solution dry on scalp. In a few days, you should notice that your loose dandruff has completely disappeared.*

### Ideas:
*You can help control dandruff by making sure you are eating the right foods, cutting back on fatty dishes, and keeping your scalp moisturized. Avoid highly detergent shampoos or alcohol-based rinses and indulge in some of the hair packs described on pages 37 and 38.*

**Yield:**    8 ounces

# Super-thick Hair and Scalp Treatments

*Treat your hair to this plumping rinse when it feels brittle and fragile or when you feel that you have to look ten years younger. It adds incredible body and fullness to the hair and leaves it soft and shiny, too.*

**2 tablespoons molasses**
**2 tablespoons unflavored gelatin**
**1 tablespoon condensed milk**
**1 tablespoon stale beer**

Combine ingredients in a small bowl, microwave on low power for 2 minutes, remove, and allow to cool before using.

### How to Use:

*Comb or brush into your hair. Cover hair with a plastic shower cap or wind a sheet of plastic wrap around your hair and cover with a thick terry cloth towel. Leave the treatment on for 30 minutes, rinse in warm water, and shampoo.*

**Yield:** 3 ounces

## Sooper Hair Soother

*Although summer is especially tough on your hair, it is also the best time to find the ingredients for a super hair soother. Try tossing 1 banana, 1 tablespoon yogurt, 1 tablespoon wheat germ oil, 1/4 ripe avocado, and 1/4 ripe cantaloupe into the blender for 1 minute. Apply the mixture at once to freshly shampooed hair, leave on for 10 minutes; shampoo again. Complete the body-building routine for your hair by shampooing with **Healthy Secret Herbal Shampoo**, page 31, and rinsing with **Sea Rinse for Damaged Hair**, page 35.*

*Idea:*

*Here's another treat that you can try for conditioning and feeding dry, brittle hair:*

*Mix a half cup of mayonnaise with a few drops of your shampoo, then add enough lukewarm water to pour. Apply to hair after a regular shampoo, leave on for 10 minutes, and then shampoo out.*

*Yield:*   4 ounces

# Avocado Scalp Treatment

*Try this "Rodeo Drive" treatment for your hair and scalp as a simple antidote to too much sun or chlorine. It is soothing, especially if you have a sunburn on your scalp.*

**1 egg**
**1/2 avocado, peeled and mashed**
**2 tablespoons wheat germ oil**

Beat egg until frothy, either in a blender or by hand. Gradually add the avocado and oil, beating until smooth. Microwave on low power for 90 seconds to warm and use immediately.

*How to Use:*

*Divide your hair into several sections and apply the paste first to the scalp and then work outward, massaging the paste along the hair shaft. Cover your head with a plastic cap and leave on for 30 minutes.*

*For an even more concentrated treatment, try warming a towel in the microwave oven for 2 minutes on high power and wrapping it over the plastic cap. This relaxing treatment helps your scalp and hair absorb the solution a bit better. To cleanse your hair, rinse first in lukewarm water for 5 minutes and then use any of the mild shampoo formulas in this chapter.*

*Yield:*   1 application

# Euro-spa Hair Restorative

*If you're fighting baldness and have all but given up, there may still be hope. Assuming that you're not one of the hundreds of thousands of sufferers of male-pattern baldness (and the numbers are actually smaller than you think) your thinning hairline problem may be reversible. Personal trainers at European spas know that for many men, baldness is a sign of either fatty deposits just under the scalp, a vitamin E deficiency, poor circulation in the scalp, or scalp and hair that are undernourished or extra dry.*

*All of these are remediable conditions. So if you notice that your hair is beginning to thin or fall out and your mother's father looks like a fully sprouted Chia Pet, the chances are you're not suffering from male pattern baldness. Try this remedy and see if it works.*

**2 tablespoons dried rosemary**
**1 1/2 teaspoons camphor**
**1 quart water**
**1 teaspoon baking soda**
**1/2 cup 100-proof vodka**

1   Grind rosemary and camphor in a food processor or in a mortar and pestle, or whirl in a blender on low power.

2   Boil water in microwave on high power for 3 minutes. Remove and add baking soda. Simmer on medium for 1 minute. Remove and pour over rosemary and camphor mixture.

3   Microwave on low/medium power for 2 minutes. Remove and let stand overnight. Strain and add vodka.

### *How to Use:*

Using a cotton ball, dab the solution around your hair roots after your shower in the morning or after a shampoo at night. At first you should use the solution only three times a week. If you notice that your scalp feels tingly and that your hair seems thicker, you can increase to four times a week.

### *Ideas:*

As your hair starts to thicken, you may want to stimulate the new growth or make what's coming in grow faster. First, try grinding 1 tablespoon dried parsley and 1 tablespoon dried rosemary leaves, microwaving them together for 90 seconds to 2 minutes on low power, letting them stand at room temperature, and then combing the dried mixture through your hair every night for six months.

You can also try microwaving 1/4 cup dried nettles in a cup of water on high power for 3 minutes and then on medium for 2 minutes, letting stand overnight, and using it as a dip for your comb. Each morning after your shower, dip your comb in the nettle juice and gently comb against the grain. You should always comb gently, because you don't want to pull out any new hairs that are just coming in and haven't had time to develop a strong root system.

### *Yield:*   36 ounces

# Lemon Hair Spray

*This hair spray is so simple to make it seems incredible that it can really work, but it really works. It also adds a bit of body to fine, limp hair, and the lemons give light hair added shine and dancing highlights, not to mention a wonderful scent.*

*Try this mixture if you like a natural look and especially like the idea of coming by it in a completely natural way.*

**2 lemons, sliced**
**2 cups hot water**

1   Place lemon slices and water in a bowl in oven and micro-wave on high power for 3 minutes or until mixture reaches a rolling boil. Reduce to medium power for 4 minutes or until the water is reduced to 1 cup. Remove and cool.

2   Line a strainer with cheesecloth and strain the mixture. Squeeze out the cloth thoroughly to get all the juice, and retain the lemon pulp for garden compost.

3   Pour the strained mixture into a pump-type container. Mixture will keep for 1 to 2 months in the refrigerator.

**Idea:**
   *If you use hair spray very rarely, try adding a few drops of your favorite cologne to the mixture to help it last a bit longer.*

**Yield:**   8 ounces

# Deep Tanning Oil

*This preparation is for those Mediterranean or southern California types who always seem to tan easily—it should not be used on children or on people with fair skin. However, if you like to sit in the sun and roast, in spite of all the health warnings to the contrary, at least slather this soothing oil all over. It really, really works to give you soft skin and a nice, even tan. It is guaranteed to work if you behave sensibly toward the sunning process: start out slowly, add a little more time each day, and reapply the oil often.*

*Remember, however, that doctors warn against repeated and extended exposure to the sun. This product, although topically soothing, does not contain any sunscreening ingredients.*

*To save money on the ingredients, I always use a leaf from my aloe plant for the gel. To extract the gel, break off a leaf near the spine of the plant and place the leaf between two sheets of plastic wrap. Roll toward the cut end with a rolling pin and scoop the gel right into the tanning mixture. One large leaf yields about 2 tablespoons of gel. Another money-saving hint is to buy your wheat germ oil from a store that sells farm or horse-grooming supplies—it's much cheaper and it's fine for topical use.*

**1/2 cup very strong tea (4 tea bags, 1/2 cup water)**
**1 cup wheat germ oil**
**1/4 cup sesame oil**
**1/4 cup apple cider vinegar**
**2 tablespoons aloe gel**
**1 teaspoon iodine**

1   Brew the tea by microwaving on high for 3 minutes and then on low for 2 minutes. Remove from the oven and allow the tea to sit for a few minutes before combining it with the rest of the ingredients.

2   Stir the oils and vinegar together. Blend in the microwave on low power for 90 seconds, remove, and gently and gradually beat in the aloe gel, using a wire whisk or wooden spoon. Add the tea and iodine and pour into a tightly capped plastic container.

3   Mixture will keep for up to 3 months in the refrigerator.

*Yield:*   16 ounces

# Fresh and Fast Tooth Potions

*The basic tooth powder and paste recipes given here work very, very well to keep your teeth bright and clean. They are as old as all of our grandmothers, of course, and there are numerous variations, some of which are listed.*

## Superwhite Tooth Powder

*Do not add salt to this basic recipe if you suspect you have an allergy to salt; otherwise, the salt is very good for the maintenance of your teeth and gums.*

**2 tablespoons lemon or orange rind**
**1/4 cup baking soda**
**2 teaspoons salt**

1   Place the orange or lemon rind in a single layer on a few absorbent paper towels and dry in the microwave for 2 minutes on medium power. Rotate the rinds and continue to dry for another 2 to 4 minutes on low power. Cool.

2   Place the dried rinds in a blender or food processor and grind until the peel is a fine powder. Add baking soda and salt and return the mixture to the microwave for 90 seconds at low power.

3   Return to blender and process for a few seconds more, or until you have a fine powder. You can also use a mortar and pestle to grind the rind, baking soda, and salt together.

***How to Use:***
*Store the powder in a large salt shaker and shake directly onto your wet toothbrush, or keep the powder in an airtight tin*

*and dip your moistened toothbrush into the mix. Brush thoroughly and rinse well.*

**Yield:** 5 ounces

# Superwhite Toothpaste

**1 teaspoon Superwhite Tooth Powder**
**1/4 teaspoon hydrogen peroxide**

Brush your teeth with the mixture, but be careful to rinse and spit out rather than swallow any of the peroxide because it could make you sick if you drink a lot of it. It will taste crummy enough, so you won't be tempted. This solution is very healing to gums and teeth, and my sister's dentist says that it keeps plaque from forming.

**Yield:** 1 application

# Instant Sweet Toothpaste

*This is a dandy homemade recipe to try if you have small children who are reluctant to brush.*

**1 teaspoon Superwhite Tooth Powder**
**1 tablespoon ripe strawberries, crushed**

Mix strawberries and powder into a paste, blend in microwave on low power for 90 seconds, remove, cool thoroughly in refrigerator for five minutes, and brush as usual. This is a much sweeter tasting toothpaste than the peroxide mixture, and it also whitens teeth over time.

**Yield:** 4 ounces

# Diuretic Diet Tea

*Even before the mudpacks and the Swedish massage, before the afternoons in rich sulfur baths or before toning up your chakra for a psychic revelation, you will have to drop those five to seven pounds of excess water you're retaining. You can accomplish this in two ways. First, you have to stop eating the foods that make you retain water. That means you'll have to cut down on salt. I recommend you cut out salt completely, replacing it with one of the salt substitutes we recommended in Chapters 3 and 6.*

*Next, you have to encourage your body to release the excess water. Mineral water or mineral water with lime is one safe and gentle way to stimulate your system, because water is a natural cleanser. Then, a diuretic tea, such as the following chamomile and rose-petal brew, is a natural way to ease water retention and put your body back on a normal healthy cycle.*

**1/4 cup fresh rose petals**
**2 tablespoons chamomile**
**2 cups boiling water**
**1 small wedge of lime**

1   Dry the rose petals by placing them in a single layer on absorbent toweling in the microwave and warming them on low power for 6 minutes. Remove the petals and grind them in a mortar and pestle or your food processor.

2   Mix dried rose petals with chamomile and grind as finely as possible.

3   Add to water and let simmer and steep in your microwave on low to medium power for 5 minutes. Remove, let stand, add wedge of lime, and drink while still hot.

### How to Use:

*I recommend drinking your tea while in a hot tub. The tea will raise your body temperature and open up your pores. If you are soaking in an herbal bath or using one of the pore-cleansing recipes described in Chapter 1, the results will be nothing short of miraculous.*

**Yield:**   16 ounces

# Bay Leaf and Vinegar Tonic

*This is a magic elixir that breaks down the fat you've ingested during the day and washes it away before your body has a chance to store it away on thighs, hips, cheeks, or upper arms. This tonic doesn't taste particularly good; in fact you'll probably have to gear yourself up to take it, but it works because the vinegar does indeed break down fat—you've seen what it does to oil in salad dressing—and bay leaf is a natural diuretic. In combination, these two ingredients help you lose fat while cleansing your body of toxins. Bay leaf and vinegar tonic is one of the secret spa recipes that Rodeo Drive habitués routinely pay hundreds of dollars a day to consume. Now you can have it for pennies in the privacy of your own spa.*

**1/2 bay leaf**
**1/4 cup white vinegar**
**1 cup water**
**1 sliver lemon or lime**

Crumble bay leaf into coarse chunks and mix with vinegar. Add to water and microwave on high power for 3 minutes, reduce to low/medium and steep for 4 minutes. Strain, add lemon or lime. Drink while still hot but not scalding.

### How to Use:

*Drink your tonic immediately before bedtime. By the following morning, you will definitely feel less bloated and your body will have rid itself of much of the fat you ingested the day before.*

*Idea:*

You can also use the vinegar, bay leaf, and water solution as a facial by soaking a soft terry face cloth with the mixture, microwaving the terry cloth on high power for 2 minutes, letting it cool slightly so it doesn't scald, and applying it immediately to your face. Let it break down the surface fat from your skin and then splash cold vinegar on your face. It will firm up your face, open up your sinus passages, and make you feel wonderful.

*Yield:*    10 ounces

# Glasnost Hot Vodka Rubdown

*Ever wonder why the Soviet athletes always run away with all the gold medals at every Olympics? The secret may be in the rubdown they get after every event. And the secret of the rubdown is in the skin treatment—the vodka and the herbal ingredients: pungent cloves, tangy mint, sweet lavender, and fragrant rose petals. This rubdown tones up muscles, cleanses the pores, tightens the skin, and refreshes all of your senses.*

*The rubdown has a vinegar base, just like the tonic in the previous recipe. Vinegar breaks down surface fat and restores the vital acid balance of the skin. This is especially important for athletes who shower a lot and can easily develop dry skin conditions if they're not careful.*

*Therefore, I recommend you use your vodka rubdown after your shower in order to get the full benefit of the vinegar treatment. The alcohol in the vodka will keep your skin nice and tight and make you look healthier all over. If you're going directly to work after your exercise session and worry about the aroma of vodka, replace it with rubbing alcohol.*

**1 tablespoon fresh rose petals**
**1/2 cup cider vinegar**
**1 tablespoon dried rosemary**
**1/2 tablespoon cloves**
**1 tablespoon dried lavender**
**2 cups water**

**1/4 cup vodka**
*or*
**Rubbing alcohol**
*or*
**Witch hazel**
**1 wedge fresh orange**
**3 tablespoons fresh mint**

1   Dry rose petals in microwave on low/medium power for 6 minutes. Combine vinegar, herbs, cloves, dried rose petals, and lavender and microwave on low/medium power for 5 minutes. Let stand for 24 hours.

2   Mix vinegar solution with water and boil in microwave on high power for 3 minutes, then reduce to medium power for 3 minutes. Let stand for 15 minutes to steep and cool.

3   Combine dried ingredients with vinegar mixture and orange. Add vodka or alcohol and store in a sterilized glass jar with a tight-fitting lid.

***How to Use:***
*Shake jar to distribute ingredients before using as either a hot or cold rubdown or splash immediately after your shower.*

***Yield:***   22 ounces

# Instant Lemon-Ginger Rubdown

*This is an executive-level treat that you can enjoy even if you're only at the mailroom level in your organization. The lemon-ginger rubdown also offers a pick-me-up between meetings or after a quick lunchtime workout.*

**2 tablespoons powdered ginger**
**2 1/4 cups lemon juice**
**2 quarts mineral water**

Microwave ginger, lemon juice, and water on high power for 3 minutes. Remove. Let cool and store in a sterilized glass jar with a tightly fitting lid in the refrigerator.

***How to Use:***
*Fill sink with very hot water and immerse a washcloth to heat. Or, dampen washcloth and microwave it on low power for 90 seconds. Sponge off with hot washcloth, reheat, and pour lemon-ginger solution onto washcloth. Rub vigorously with the cloth and rinse.*

*For an especially invigorating experience, wash off with hot water, use a loofah to remove dead skin, then use washcloth permeated with lemon-ginger solution, and rinse.*

***Yield:***   82 ounces

# Gritty Scrub Hand Cleaner

*This is one of the best ideas in the world, as far as I'm concerned, because it cleverly solves the problem of what to do with all those infernal slices of leftover soap that no one, not even James Michener, can ever bear to throw away. I once read an article about how the fabulously successful writer of those universe-sized sagas keeps a plastic margarine container filled with soap slivers, just waiting to be reborn, in his guest bathroom for all the world to see. So don't be embarrased if you save soap slivers, too. It might just be a function of genius, after all.*

**Several small bits and pieces (about 1 cup)
of soap, thoroughly dried
1 cup cornmeal
1/4 cup almonds
4 tablespoons corn oil**

1   Break up soap into chunks and feed into a food processor or blender and whirl until the soap is granulated. Add the cornmeal and almonds and continue to process until you have a fine meal.

2   Blend meal with the corn oil by stirring and microwaving on low power for 90 seconds. Repeat cycle until you have a paste smooth enough for the container of your choice. If you want to store the paste in a plastic margarine tub with a lid, the paste should be semisolid. If you want to pour the hand cleaner into a pump-type dispenser, add more oil until the right consistency is reached.

*Yield:*   18 ounces

# Soft Soaps

*Here is the soap that is good for everything, depending on how you vary or customize it. You will find references to Soft Soap throughout* **Zapcrafts**—*use it in the plain, basic formula for simple washing of delicate items and for adding to other recipes. Add scent for personal use—spritz some in the tub as the water is running, and add oils if you would like softer-feeling skin.*

*If you don't have enough bits of soap collected to make* **Soft Soap***, you can add soap flakes to make 1 cup, but do begin your collection of soap slivers right away—see page 53 for another use for them.*

## Basic Supersaver Soft Soap

**Several bits, slivers, and pieces of
used soap—enough to make 1 cup, dried out,**
*or*
**1 cup soap flakes
1 cup hot water**

1   If you are using soap bits, grind them to a fine powder in your food processor or blender. Mix with the soap flakes, if necessary, to make 1 cup.

2   Pour hot water over the soap, microwave on high power for 90 seconds to bring to a boil, remove, and stir until soap is completely dissolved. Cool thoroughly before using.

3   Label and store in a pump-type dispenser or a squeeze-top plastic container.

**Yield:**   8 ounces

# Scented Soft Soap

**Several drops essential oil**
*or*
**Your favorite perfume**
**1 cup Basic Supersaver Soft Soap (page 54)**

Mix and store as described for **Basic Supersaver Soft Soap**.

*Yield:*  8 ounces

# Rich Soft Soap

**2 tablespoons olive, wheat germ,**
*or*
**Almond oil**
**1 cup Basic Supersaver Soft Soap (page 54)**
*or*
**Scented Soft Soap**

Warm the oil in your microwave on low power for 2 minutes and beat gradually into the soap, using a blender or an electric mixer to make sure oil is distributed evenly; mix and store as described for **Basic Supersaver Soft Soap.**

*Yield:*  8 ounces

# Athlete's Friction Bath

*Hot friction baths are an ideal way to tone muscles after a workout or at the end of a trying, taxing day. There are a variety of combinations of herbs and spices you can use to stimulate and relax. Following are some of my favorites. The basic recipe consists of a mixture of witch hazel, rosewater, and dried rose petals. To that basic mixture you can add juniper berries, honey, chamomile, linseed oil, lavender, ginger, or sage (see **Variations**).*

*Try these friction lotions as rubdowns before the bath or add them to a very hot bath for the complete spa bath treatment. After you've tried a few of the suggested combinations, experiment with some of your own mixtures, too.*

**1 cup dried or fresh rose petals**
**1/4 cup witch hazel**
**4 cups water**
**1/2 cup rosewater**

1   If using fresh rose petals, dry them in the microwave by lightly layering them on a few sheets of absorbent toweling and warming on medium power for 4 to 5 minutes. Stir and continue drying for 5 minutes more. Combine with witch hazel and let stand for 10 minutes.

2   Microwave water until boiling, remove, let cool, and add witch-hazel mixture and rosewater. Store mixture in the refrigerator in a sterilized glass jar with a tightly fitting lid.

***How to Use:***
*Add to hot bath water and soak for 15 minutes.*

*You can also infuse hot towels with the witch-hazel mixture and give yourself a vigorous rubdown before your bath.*

### Variations:

To your witch-hazel mixture you can add juniper berries and warm the solution in the microwave on medium power for 2 minutes. Add to bath water.

Add ground ginger to your witch-hazel mixture for a spicy, invigorating bath.

Add dried lavender petals and cinnamon for a soft, refreshing, lightly scented bath.

Add sage and basil for an invigorating friction bath.

Thyme and bay leaves added to the witch-hazel mixture in a bath just before bedtime will help you leave all of the worries of the day behind in the bathwater and guarantee you a sound sleep.

Spearmint leaves and mint extract added to the witch-hazel mixture will give you a vigorous start to the day.

Sage, thyme, lavender, sea salt or kosher salt, vinegar, and garlic will give a soothing rubdown bath either in the evening or after a workout.

Oatmeal or rolled oats added to the witch-hazel mixture will remove dry skin and help relieve chafing and itching during hot summer months.

Pine oil with rosemary will help both men and women get to sleep faster on cold, wintry nights.

**Yield:** 38 ounces

# Rich and Soothing Milk Bath

*Here are two different spa baths, combined into one interesting and luxurious experience. You will want to use this skin-soothing bath often, or at least as often as you can afford.*

**2 cups honey**
**3 quarts buttermilk**
**1 cup bicarbonate of soda**
**1 cup kosher or sea salt**
**1 quart bottled mineral water**

1   Microwave the honey on high power for 90 seconds, remove, and mix in with the milk in a big glass bowl or jar. Microwave milk and honey on medium power for 3 minutes or until all the honey is dissolved.

2   Fill a tub with water as hot as you can stand and add the soda, salt, and mineral water. Then add half of the milk and honey mixture.

### How to Use:
*Soak in bath for 5 minutes. Gradually add the remaining portion of the milk and honey as you loofah away the top layer of dead skin and replenish vital oils with the milk and honey mixture.*

### Idea:
*For an even more luxurious bath, add one bottle of flat champagne to the milk and honey mixture.*

**Yield:**   1 gallon bath solution

# Herbal Air Spray for the At-home Spa

*Although you prepare all of your spa items in your microwave, you will use them in the privacy of your bath. The effectiveness of your bathroom health spa, whether it's in an Upper West Side New York City apartment or in a ranch house in a suburb of Indianapolis, comes from the bouquet of sweet herbs or pungent spices. Use this simple mixture to scent and cleanse the air of smoky or musty odors. Experiment with the herbs and spices that smell the nicest to you—remember that it's your own space that you're improving—and choose a combination that makes you feel good.*

*You might try scenting your air to produce a special effect: rosemary is supposed to ward off evil spirits, cinnamon smells like a bakery, and pine reminds the nose of Christmas.*

*You can save money by infusing herbs or teas that you suspect to be buggy or too weak to cook with, or save the peelings from apples or lemons and add them to your brew.*

*Plan to keep an open container handy for adding to your collection of items for this potpourri, and for an especially clever way to store your waiting collection, see the **Idea** that follows.*

**2 cups white vinegar**
**Any combination of the following**
**herbs or spices (dried or fresh),**
**to make 1 cup:**

**rosemary, lavender, cloves, rose petals,**
**thyme, cinnamon sticks, pine needles,**
**apple, orange, lemon, or lime peel,**

**honeysuckle or other fragrant blossoms,
peppermint, walnut, or vanilla extract**

1   Place selected ingredients in a glass bowl. Microwave on medium power for 3 minutes and then on low/medium for 3 minutes. Cool.

2   Pour liquid and herbs into a large, sturdy jar. Close jar tightly, label, and store it where you will see it for 2 to 4 weeks. Remember to shake the jar once or twice a week.

3   Strain and reserve juice. Pour liquid into a pump-type spray container or atomizer. Label container.

***Idea:***
  *Take a cup or so of your dried ingredients and pour them into an oven mitt. Sew up the opening with basting stitches and use the scented mitt for a hot plate—fragrance will be released every time you use it and you can recycle the dried materials into* **Herbal Air Spray** *when you are ready to wash the mitt.*

***Yield:***   16 ounces

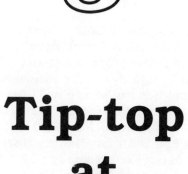

# Tip-top
# at
# Top Speed

*Zap away those post holiday blahs and boardroom jitters, or simply zap yourself back to health the quick and easy way by preparing these home-brewed remedies in your microwave. Microwaving them saves you time and money. Remember that the faster you're back on your feet and moving and shaking the world around you, the better your chances to outrun the next flu bug that stalks.*

# *Recipes and Instructions*

# Nighttime Adult Cold Remedy

*This remedy is guaranteed to let you sleep through your common cold symptoms just as soundly as the store-bought kind, and it tastes better, too. It has no real medicinal claims, unless you, like many people, believe that a good night's sleep is all you need to cure your common cold.*

**1/4 cup water**
**1 lemon**
**1/4 cup maple syrup**
**2 tablespoons brandy**

1   Microwave water in a cup on high power for 2 minutes and remove.

2  Squeeze all the juice from the lemon and stir it into the maple syrup. Add the syrup and brandy to the hot water and microwave on low power for 90 seconds.

3   Remove and let stand while you inhale the vapors as deeply as you can. When cool enough to drink, drink deeply, inhaling as you go. Use entire recipe and climb right into bed. This remedy works fast.

*Tip:*
   *Bundle yourself up in your warmest pajamas, turn on the electric blankets and heating pad, slowly sip the **Nighttime Adult Cold Remedy** while it's good and hot, instead of downing it in one heavy gulp, and go to sleep for 8 hours. If cold symptoms persist, see a doctor.*

*Yield:*  6 ounces

# Sweet Solution Cough Syrup

*Here is a soothing throat remedy that works for roughness brought on by too much exertion, be it from singing, shouting, hedging your puts and calls, or running around Battery Park in the coldest weather.*

**1 lemon**
**1 tablespoon glycerin**
**1/2 cup honey**

1   In a glass bowl, cover the entire lemon with water and microwave on high for 3 minutes or until water is boiling. Remove, and while still hot, slice the lemon in half and squeeze all the juice into another bowl. Remove the seeds.

2   Stir in the glycerin and honey and microwave on low power for 90 seconds to blend; let cool and store the syrup in a sterilized glass jar, tightly capped, in the pantry or bathroom. If the syrup becomes too cold, warm it by microwaving on low power for 90 seconds. The syrup will keep for 1 to 2 months.

**Tip:**
*If you have an annoying cough that occasionally keeps you up at night, simply keep a jar of honey and a spoon at your bedside and slowly suck on a spoonful of honey when the urge to cough comes upon you. The cough will magically go away.*

**Yield:**   5 ounces

# Expectorant Cough Syrup

*Here's a cough syrup remedy that is as old as the common cold—and it helps clear up some of the congestion associated with coughs and colds. The honey is also quite soothing to the throat. Remember, however, what they say on the bottles of cough syrup that you buy in the store: If a cough persists or gets worse, see your doctor.*

**2 tablespoons diced onion**
**1/2 cup honey**

1   Mix the ingredients in a glass bowl and microwave on low/medium power for 10 minutes, rotate, and then microwave on low power for 30 minutes. Strain the mixture through a coffee filter or cheesecloth and discard the onion pulp.

2   Allow the syrup to come to room temperature before using, and store at room temperature for 1 to 2 months.

### *How to Use:*

*Adults should take 1 to 2 tablespoons every 4 hours. If cough persists, or if there is a fever, call the doctor.*

*For a child between the ages of 8 and 15, take 1 teaspoon every 4 hours. For a child younger than 8 who seems ill with a cough, you should probably call a doctor rather than try home remedies.*

**Yield:**   5 ounces

# Sunflower Cough Syrup for Grown-ups

*Since this preparation contains a generous amount of gin, take it only if you can handle this ingredient. Do not attempt to take this solution when you might be called upon to drive or to operate a machine. But once you are safe at home, relax and let the syrup do its job.*

**1/2 cup sunflower seeds**
**5 cups water**
**3/4 cup gin**
**1/2 cup sugar**

1   In a glass bowl in the microwave boil the sunflower seeds in the water on high power for 4 minutes and then on medium for an additional 4 minutes or until the water is reduced to approximately 2 cups.  Strain the juice, discarding the seeds.

2   Stir in the gin and sugar and store in a tightly capped container.

### How to Use:

*For those coughs and colds that you want to treat yourself, take 1 to 2 teaspoons four times a day until you feel better. If you have a severe cough, fever, or if your symptoms worsen, discontinue all remedies and make sure you see your doctor.*

**Yield:**   22 ounces

# Jiffy Remedies for Scratchy Throats

*Wintertime sore and scratchy throats are nagging remind-ers that we're just on the edge of a cold. Scratchy throats can linger for days or even weeks, keeping us awake at night and throbbing in the morning on our way to work. Most of the time minor sore throat pain can be alleviated without heavy doses of vile-tasting syrups that wipe out our taste buds for the rest of the day.*

*Try some of these "Old Country" remedies and be sure to pass along the best of them to friends. Remember the old Ukrainian adage that applies to sore throats: "Whatever goes around comes around." Also remember that sore throats are indicators that something else may be wrong. If your sore throat persists for more than three days or gets progressively worse, call your doctor.*

**1 cup water**
**Any of the following:**
**1 tablespoon kosher salt**
*or*
**1 tablespoon dried rosemary or chamomile**
*or*
**1 tablespoon dried sage**
*or*
**1/2 cup apple cider vinegar**

If using kosher salt, mix salt in cup of water, microwave on low/medium power for 3 minutes, let cool, and gargle.

If using rosemary or chamomile, microwave cup of water on high power for 3 minutes until boiling. Remove and let stand. Steep rosemary or chamomile in the water until the water is almost black-brown. Gargle and then drink.

If using sage, microwave cup of water on high power for 3 minutes until boiling. Remove and let stand. Steep sage in cup until water turns deep green or brown. Drink tea, letting it trickle on the painful areas.

If using cider vinegar, microwave cup of water on high power for 3 minutes, or until boiling. Remove and let stand. Add apple cider vinegar and gargle. Drink remaining brew.

*Yield:* 8 ounces

# Nighttime Fever Reducer

*If you've had a bad sunburn or a reaction to insect bites, the chances are you'll run a low-grade fever for an evening or two. One way to reduce that fever is to drink a glassful of this natural solution. It will soothe you all over and reduce your fever to make you feel more comfortable. Use topical ointments for pain of sunburn or insect bites.*

**1 1/2 teaspoons cream of tartar**
**1/2 teaspoon lemon juice**
**1/2 teaspoon honey**
**2 cups water**

1   Combine all ingredients in a bowl; stir.

2   Microwave on low/medium power for 3 minutes. Cool if necessary until solution is comfortable to swallow.

### How to Use:
*Drink one glassful slowly, wait 30 minutes, and check temperature. If fever is still elevated, reheat the remaining glassful and sip slowly. If fever persists, call a doctor the next morning.*

**Yield:**   12 ounces

# Cajun Lotion

*Gulf fishermen have long had a secret muscle liniment recipe that soothes aching arms and legs after a hard day at sea. Try it for yourself and see how quickly it eases jogger's cramp or tennis player's shoulder: I gar-on-tee!*

**1 tablespoon ground cayenne pepper**
**1 pint apple cider vinegar**

1   Combine pepper and vinegar in glass bowl. Microwave on high power for 3 minutes until mixture is boiling. Reduce to medium for 3 minutes to simmer.

2   Bottle liquid while it is still hot. Let cool, but rewarm slightly by microwaving on low power for 2 minutes just before use.

### How to Use:
*Apply warm liniment directly to affected muscles as needed. As the hot cayenne pepper penetrates to aching muscles, you may want to apply a warm towel to retain some of the heat. You may also want to soak the towel in the liniment and heat in microwave on low power for 2 minutes.*

**Yield:**   16 ounces

# Swedish Spa Bath for Charley Horse

*For whatever reason, the Swedes seem to know how to take care of themselves. Maybe it's the climate! This Swedish remedy has been used by athletic teams and trainers around the country. It's a simple folk recipe for easing strained and tired muscles that have been overworked and underloved.*

**Fresh gingerroot
1 pint mineral water**

1   Grind up or grate 2 teaspoons of fresh ginger and add to water.

2   Microwave on high power for 3 minutes until brew reaches a rolling boil and reduce to medium power for 2 minutes. Let stand to steep while water turns a deep yellow. If necessary, you can urge the brew by microwaving on low until the color changes.

3   Add the brew to a hot bath.

*How to Use:*
    Soak in ginger bath for 15 to 20 minutes, making sure to work your sore muscles as gently as possible through the water.

*Yield:*   16 ounces

# Asian Foot Remedy

*For thousands of years, Asian cultures have understood that when the feet are comfortable and soothed, the entire body relaxes. Modern medicine confirms that there are so many nerve endings in the feet that even a little foot comfort goes a long way toward easing stress and reducing tension.*

*Here's a simple foot soak that you can use every night before bed to guarantee yourself a sound, trouble-free sleep. It will also make life easier for you if you have to spend a lot of time on your feet during the day.*

**Handful of kosher or coarse salt**
**1 cup white vinegar**
**1 pint water**

1   Combine salt and vinegar in water.

2   Microwave on medium power for 1 minute and then on low for 2 minutes, until solution is warm but not too hot.

### How to Use:
*Soak both feet in the solution until you feel relaxed and warm all over. Pat feet dry or wrap in soft towel and leave covered. Repeat after 2 hours if necessary.*

**Yield:**   24 ounces

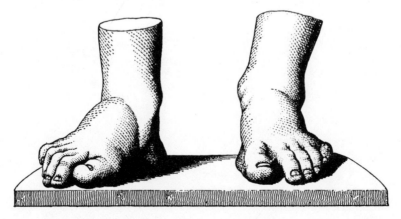

# Instant Cure for Earache

*This old Eastern European remedy for earaches works on a very simple principle: a warm compress that retains heat for long periods. The soothing heat draws blood to the infected area to carry off the toxins that are causing the pain.*

**Handful of uncooked bran
Handful of kosher salt
Small muslin or thick cloth bag**

1   Combine bran and salt in bag and seal.

2   Microwave on low/medium power for 4 minutes. Check for heat and repeat cycle until compress is clearly warm to the touch. Don't burn or overheat.

### *How to Use:*

*Lie back in a chair and apply the bag to your sore ear. Keep the bag in place until the soothing heat begins to ease the pain. If bag becomes too cool, reheat in microwave and repeat the process until your ear feels better. Remember, an ear infection that persists is a symptom of an underlying virus or injury. Be sure to call your doctor if the pain persists for more than a day.*

**Yield:**   1 treatment

# Jiffy Insect Repellant

*This recipe uses natural herbs and spices to keep pesky mosquitos and flies from dive-bombing you on otherwise pleasant summer evenings. We don't want to kill the little nasties, just send them off in other directions.*

**1/8 cup dried sage
or
1/4 cup dried rosemary
8 fresh garlic cloves
1 cup sesame or safflower oil**

1  Add sage or rosemary and garlic cloves, finely chopped, to oil.

2  Microwave on high power for 3 minutes, until liquid reaches a rolling boil. Reduce to medium for 4 minutes to simmer and thicken liquid.

3  Remove, let cool, bottle, and let settle for 1 to 2 weeks. Strain liquid before use and bottle in small sterilized containers.

### How to Use:

*Apply oil liberally to sensitive areas. You can also use it as a soothing, topical remedy after you've received insect bites.*

**Yield:**  8 ounces

# Chapped Skin Miracle Solution

*I really love this product because it has instantly healed my winter-rough, chapped hands. It's also great whenever you've overworked your hands, your elbows, your feet—it makes all your skin as smooth as a baby's. It's not a disappearing cream, however, so plan to cover your hands with cotton gloves overnight if you intend to slather it on.*

*To avoid having wind-roughened lips, try smoothing this mixture on before, during, and after exposure to the elements. It's an extremely soothing and protective cover, so you might spread some on other parts of the body exposed to cold or wind—cheeks, nose—and on your hands before you put on your gloves.*

**2 tablespoons paraffin**
**1/2 cup petroleum jelly**
**Few drops oil of lemon or other scent (optional)**

1   In a glass bowl in the microwave on low/medium power, melt the paraffin slowly in 2-minute cycles, stirring between cycles, until completely melted.

2   Add the petroleum jelly, stirring until completely combined. Microwave on low/medium power for 2 minutes. Remove from oven and add the scent, if desired.

3   Pour while salve is still liquid into a container with a snug-fitting lid. For carrying convenience, you can pour a small amount of the salve into a tiny pillbox or fancy tin.

*Yield:*   5 ounces

# Sea Salt Seasoning

*Many people are advised to eliminate or to cut back on their salt intake. Here is one easy way to achieve that difficult goal—use this concoction in place of salt at the table. You can vary and experiment with the spices listed here, but these ingredients will give a dependable tang and zip to your food. Whenever possible, use the freshest of ingredients and flash-dry them in your microwave so that your substitute salt is as spicy as possible.*

**1 cup fresh parsley**
**1 cup fresh basil**
**1/2 cup sea salt**
**2 tablespoons dried paprika**
**1 teaspoon dried oregano**
**1 teaspoon dried thyme**
**1 teaspoon black pepper**
**1 teaspoon dried marjoram**
**1 teaspoon celery seed**
**1 teaspoon garlic powder**
**1/2 teaspoon Curry in a Hurry (page 149)**
**1/2 teaspoon cayenne**

1   Dry parsley and basil by placing on a sheet of absorbent toweling and microwaving on medium power for 3 to 5 minutes.

2   Mix remaining ingredients and cook in the microwave for 90 seconds on low power.

3   Transfer to blender; blend until herbs are finely ground and well combined. Store in a tightly covered jar on the pantry shelf. Seasoning will keep well for up to 6 months.

*Yield:*   6 1/2 ounces

# Good Digestion Tea

*Try this tea when you've indulged too heavily at the table. Relax, sit back, kick off your shoes, and let this good brew be good to you.*

**2 tablespoons fresh peppermint leaves**
**1 tablespoon dried rosemary**
**1 tablespoon dried comfrey leaves**

1   Dry pepperment in the microwave oven on high/medium power for 2 minutes, taking care that leaves don't burn.

2   Blend herbs and microwave on low power for 90 seconds. Store in an airtight container.

### How to Use:

*Microwave 1 tablespoon of the tea in 1 cup of water on high power for 3 minutes, and let steep in standing tea water for 2 more minutes.*

**Yield:**   2 ounces

# Hoppy Hair Help

*Beer shampoo is healthy for your hair because it is mild and doesn't clog hair and scalp with extra soapy suds. Many professionals routinely cut their in-store shampoos with beer for precisely this reason.*

*Beer also brings up hair's natural highlights. The trick is not to pour the beer directly on your head, but to boil off the alcohol and use only the yeast and hops residues. It also helps to use the shampoo while it is still warm, so that blood flow to scalp and hair will be stimulated.*

**1 cup beer**
**1 cup shampoo**

1   Microwave beer on high power for 4 minutes, until it reaches a rolling boil.

2   Stir in shampoo and warm at medium power for 5 minutes, until the liquid has been reduced by about a third. Let cool until warm but not hot.

### How to Use:
*Use as you would any regular shampoo: Apply directly to wet scalp; lather, rinse, repeat. Rinse thoroughly.*

### Idea:
*If you save some of the beer residue, you can use it as a setting lotion after your shampoo.*

**Yield:**   16 ounces

# Fast and Fancy Crafts for Adults

*The microwave oven is a great help when creating many simple or slightly advanced craft items for the home because the quick and even heat works much better than the slower heating process of a conventional oven for drying flowers or curing craft clay items. Because the microwave works so quickly and requires little tending, a delicate piece of jewelry or flower arrangement has a much better chance of surviving the drying-out process.*

# *Recipes and Instructions*

# Homemade Paper

*I've always loved fancy and unusual papers, and I was happy to learn how easy it is to master the basic skill of making some of my own for special occasions. I've even found that "mistakes" that are too coarse or crumbly to write on have a place in art projects—I've kept all the bits and pieces of my experiments and found interesting ways to include them in other designs or, at the very least, shred them back into new paper projects.*

*The type of paper you shred will determine the shade and consistency of the final product, so choose tissue paper, old wrapping paper, interesting mail, and other odds and ends of paper with the final look in mind. Don't worry about any writing or ink on the papers—you can bleach the pulp if you think the ink darkens the color too much.*

*Once you've mastered the art of making pulp from shredded paper, you may want to try other materials for papermaking. A few ideas to get you started are listed under* **Variations**.

*Because the process is somewhat involved, I've listed the equipment you will need as well as the raw ingredients. By all means, organize your workspace and invite any children who might be milling about the house to lend a hand. They will love helping with this project.*

**4 cups shredded scrap paper**
**Food coloring or Nature's Colors (page 90)**
**2 tablespoons liquid laundry starch**
**Laundry bleach (optional)**
**Newspapers**
**Iron**

**1 window screen**
**2 large sheets of blotting paper**
**Quantity of paper toweling**

1   Put 1 cup of the shredded paper into a blender. Pour between 1 and 2 cups of hot water and 1 tablespoon of laundry starch over the paper. Cover, and process until you have a thick pulp. Add extra color, if desired, or a few drops of laundry bleach if the color seems too dark.

2   Pour the pulp into a large bowl and process the rest of the paper in the same way, 1 cup at a time, adding the additional pulp to the bowl until all the paper is processed into a pulpy mush that is the consistency of thin oatmeal or gruel. Mix more hot water into the pulp if it seems too thick, and make sure you add color at this stage if you don't like the shade of the pulp.

3   Organize your work space next to the bowl by first covering the area with several thicknesses of newspaper. Plug in the iron and turn it on the woolen or warm setting. Place the window screen directly over the newspapers and spoon some of the pulp onto the screen. Smooth it around evenly and let some of the moisture drip out of the paper. Press the pulp gently with the back of the spoon.

4   Cover the pulp on the screen with a piece of the blotting paper, flip the screen, pulp, and paper over onto fresh newspaper covered with paper toweling, and carefully lift off the screen, leaving the pulp sitting on the blotting paper.

5   Cover the pulp with another piece of blotting paper and change the newspaper underneath if it's too wet. Place the pulp layer (along with the newspaper) onto a microwave-safe tray and heat for 2 minutes on medium power. Check for dampness, turn, and microwave for 2 more minutes on medium, if necessary. Paper should be only slightly damp.

6   Iron the blotting-paper sandwich, moving the iron slowly and gently over the blotting paper. Lift a corner every now and then to see how well your paper is coming along—the paper is ready when you can lift off the top blotter and peel the new paper off the bottom blotter. Iron until the paper is dry enough to peel.

7   Let the blotting paper dry out completely between ironings (about 1 hour) and then spoon out more pulp onto the screen. Repeat Steps 3, 4, 5, and 6 until all the pulp is used.

### Variations:

*Try adding exotic items to the shredded paper in your blender. My children have made paper from celery, banana skins, and scraps of blue jeans that have soaked overnight in 1/2 cup of laundry bleach.*

### How to Use:

*You can use the variously shaped patches of paper just as they come from the blotting papers, but you can and should trim the papers with a paper cutter or scissors for a more refined look.*

*Try adding a deckle edge to your paper by marking a straight line where you want the edge to be and then dabbing along that line with a brush or Q-tip dipped in water. Once the line is nice and wet, you can work it apart with your fingers. Let it dry completely before using. You can tint the edge another shade by using watercolors in place of plain water.*

*Many artists are making whole constructions from home-made paper. Try draping a piece of still-damp paper over an interesting shape and letting it dry for a special effect.*

**Yield:**  10 to 20 sheets

# Instant Crafty Clay

*This mixture creates the finest texture of all the different types of craft doughs. It also hardens by air drying rather than baking, so any features or fine details that you've created will not puff up in the oven. Interesting effects can be created by coloring this clay before working with it—see **Ideas** for more information.*

**2 cups baking soda**
**1 cup cornstarch**
**1 1/2 cups water**

## Optional Ingredients

**Food coloring or Nature's Colors (page 90)**
**Oil of cloves or peppermint extract**

## For Finishing

**Matte acrylic varnish**

1   Combine baking soda and cornstarch in a microwave-safe bowl and add the water. Add coloring and pepperment extract (for a more pleasant scent), if desired. Stir to blend completely. Microwave on medium power for 3 minutes. Mixture will become thin and smooth at first. Remove and stir again.

2   Microwave again on medium power for 3 minutes, stir, and repeat cycle until mixture is too thick to stir. Turn the mixture out onto a cookie sheet to cool, covering with a damp cloth. When cool, knead until smooth.

3   Store the mixture in a tightly closed plastic bag in the refrigerator for up to 2 weeks.

### How to Use:

*Items can be molded from this clay by either shaping with your hands, rolling out and cutting with a cookie cutter, or pushing through a cookie or garlic press.*

*Clay will harden at room temperature; the time required will depend on the size of the object. Most items are dry after 24 hours, and if necessary, you can finish drying the pieces in your microwave by warming them for 90-second cycles on low to medium power. Keep a close watch that the clay doesn't overcook, and turn the pieces occasionally.*

### Idea:

*Consider tinting the **Instant Crafty Clay** with different spices from your kitchen for a simple, earthy look. Try using dry mustard for a creamy color, or cinnamon and allspice for darker tones.*

### Hints:

*Smooth off any rough edges after drying with an emery board.*

*Because this clay is especially absorbent, more than one coat of varnish or shellac will be necessary. Experiment with a trial piece to see how many coats you will need—I've used as many as five coats on a thick figure.*

**Yield:**   20 ounces

# Microwave Molding Dough

*This craft dough is very pliable and simple to make and use. Some of the ingredients listed are not strictly necessary—just nice. The powdered alum retards spoilage and the cooking oil makes the dough a little easier to work with, but if you don't have these items handy, or if you're just beginning to experiment with this craft form, just go ahead and make up the dough with flour, salt, and water.*

**4 cups unsifted flour
1 cup salt
1 1/2 cups water**

## *Optional Ingredients*

**1 tablespoon powdered alum
1 tablespoon cooking oil
1/4 teaspoon food coloring
*or*
Nature's Colors (page 90)
1/4 teaspoon oil of cloves
*or*
Peppermint extract**

## *For Finishing*

**Acrylic paints
Spray acrylic fixative
*or*
Clear or orange shellac**

1   Mix together flour, salt, and alum if you are using it. With a big wooden spoon, slowly stir in the water, oil, and, if you are using them, coloring, and scent. Keep mixing until the dough follows the spoon around the bowl and then knead with your hands until smooth. This initial kneading will only take a minute or two to get the dough going and to make it pliable. After that, you will knead as you work with smaller pieces and the dough will stay soft.

2   Transfer the dough to a plastic container with a tight-fitting lid or to a plastic bag. Store dough in the refrigerator until ready to use. It will remain in good condition for up to 4 weeks. Let it warm to room temperature before using.

### How to Use:

*Generously flour the work surface and pinch off just enough dough to mold with. Leave the rest in the plastic bag or container until needed. Fill a small bowl with water to use as glue when you want to stick two pieces together.*

*When you have made an item you want to keep, place it on a floured, flat microwave sheet and microwave on low/ medium power for at least 30 minutes. Baking time varies considerably, depending on the thickness of the object. It's a good idea to check for doneness by inserting a toothpick into the thickest part of the item. When the toothpick comes out clean, the ornament is done. If you think your ornaments are getting too brown, cover them with brown wrapping paper, and compensate by cooking a bit longer.*

*After the item is completely dry, you can paint it with acrylic paints and then either paint it with shellac or spray it with several coats of acrylic fixative.*

### Ideas:

*This dough is used quite successfully for creating homey-looking Christmas ornaments. When my kids were little, I helped them make their own creations each year for the tree, and now I treasure these ornaments most of all.*

*Try helping children create their own handprints by stretching out their hands on a 1/2-inch-thick layer of dough while you carefully cut around their fingers with a dull paring knife. Or, the children can press their handprints into a plaque-size circle of dough.*

*All sorts of kitchen implements can be used to give artistic textures to the dough. By far the most interesting effects can be created by forcing the dough through a garlic press. The resultant threads can become a bird's nest, hair, animal fur, or, of course, spaghetti. Just remember to "glue" the strands together with water as you go. Add teeny little eggs to a nest or roll out some meatballs for a bowl of spaghetti.*

*Another natural creation for* **Microwave Molding Dough** *is to make a bread basket and fill it with bagels, or even pretend muffins. To make a basket, roll out and cut thick strips of dough. Drape several, close together, across an inverted, microwave-safe baking dish. Weave strips in the opposite direction through the original ones. Create a lattice-work design and finish off the edges as if you were creating a fancy pie. Bake your creation, dish and all, in the oven, and lift the basket off the dish when it is completely cool.*

### *Hints:*

*A rolling pin is extremely useful for flattening the dough, but if you have many little hands around the table at once, cans of soup or vegetables will work just as well.*

*You can finish the smaller items by coating them with clear nail polish. Or try brushing them with evaporated milk if you want your creations to look brown and golden, like baked goods.*

If you want to add a hanger for a Christmas ornament or wall plaque, push a paper clip almost all the way into the top of the ornament.

To create a hole for threading a pendant, take a cocktail straw and carefully drill out the hole just before you are ready to bake.

In the hands of a real craft artist, the various dough mixtures described in this chapter can turn into true works of art. For those with an amateur's enthusiasm, here is an easy project that can turn into a nice conversation piece. Remove the crusts from a slice of white bread and place the bread in a shallow bowl to which you've added 2 teaspoons water, a drop of red food color, and a squirt or two of white glue. Mush and knead the bread and break off a small piece. Mash and smush it between your fingers until you have a flat piece that looks like a rose petal. Continue and make enough petals for a complete rose.

Dry the pieces by warming in the microwave on low to medium power for 2-minute cycles, glue the pieces together, and glue on a little ribbon loop, and you have an interesting pendant.

**Yield:** 40 ounces

# Nature's Colors

*These colors have all the softness and variety of the colors you find in nature—and they are all safe and nontoxic for any use. The colors will fade with time, however, so if you want a dye to be permanent you will probably want to work with either food coloring, tempera paints, or acrylics, depending on the project.*

*If you would like to try natural colors for dyeing yarns or woolens, refer to the **Hints** that follow for information about making these colors last through the laundry process. You can store these natural colors in the refrigerator for up to 2 weeks.*

## *Red*

**1 cup fresh or canned beets**
**Water to cover**
**2 teaspoons vinegar**
*or*
**1 cup cranberries**
**Water to cover**

If using fresh beets, cover them with water in an enamel or glass pan, and cook on high power in the microwave for 3 to 5 minutes, or until water boils and beets are barely done. Remove the beets and peel, slice, and chop them, reserving the juice. Return beets to the juice and soak them for 4 hours. Strain liquid and measure out 3/4 cup. Add the vinegar to the liquid.

If using canned beets, strain out 3/4 cup of their liquid into a glass bowl and add 2 teaspoons of vinegar. Boil in the microwave on high power for 2 minutes.

If using cranberries, cover with water and microwave on high power for 3 minutes to bring to a boil, then reduce to medium for 5 minutes, mashing the cranberries as they soften. Repeat the medium cycle, mash cranberries, and microwave on medium power for 3 more minutes. Remove and strain liquid.

## *Yellow*

**Outer skins of 5 yellow onions**
**1 cup water**
*or*
**1 cup daffodil, acacia, or crocus blossoms**
**Water to cover**

If using yellow onions, microwave the dark, dry outer skins in the water on high power in a covered glass pan for 3 minutes, or until the liquid is dark yellow. Strain the juice.

If using flower blossoms, cover with water in a glass pan, microwave on high power for 3 minutes or until boiling; cover, reduce to low/medium power for 25 minutes. Strain liquid.

## *Blue*

**1/2  head red cabbage, chopped**
**1 cup water**
*or*
**1/2 cup fresh or canned blueberries**
**Water to cover**

If using cabbage, microwave it in the water in a covered glass pan on medium/low power for at least 15 minutes, or until the cabbage turns dark green and is just tender. Strain the juice, which will be blue.

For a darker shade of blue, cover fresh blueberries with water and microwave on medium power for 15 minutes. Mash the berries and strain the juice. If using canned blueberries, strain their juice, warm on low to medium power for 3 to 5 minutes, strain again.

# *Purple*

**1/2 cup fresh or frozen blackberries**

Use the pulp directly by microwaving frozen blackberries at defrost or low power for 10 minutes and then blending for 30 seconds. Strain and use the juice.

# *Green*

**Outer skins of 5 red onions**
**1 cup water**
*or*
**1 cup grass clippings, spinach, or moss**
**Water to cover**

If using onions, microwave the outer skins in the water in a covered glass pan on high power for 3 minutes to bring to a boil and then on medium power for 4 minutes. Strain the juice.

If using grass, spinach, or moss, cover with water and microwave on high power in a glass pan for 1 minute and then on medium, covered, for 3 minutes. Strain the liquid.

# *Brown*

**1 cup coffee grounds or 10 tea bags**
**1 cup water**

Cover coffee grounds with water or add tea bags to water. Microwave on high power, uncovered, in a glass pan for 3 minutes, then reduce to medium power for 5 minutes while the liquid simmers. Remove and strain the liquid.

### *Hints:*

*If you plan on using any of the above colors on fabrics, you will have to boil the fabric in a fixer or mordant before adding the colors. There are several different types of mordant you can use, and each will give a different shade when mixed with the dye. You will have to experiment to get the exact shade you like. You can choose either 4 tablespoons of potassium alum mixed with 1 tablespoon cream of tartar, or 1 teaspoon of chrome mixed with 1 1/2 teaspoons cream of tartar.*

*To apply mordant to fabric, first dissolve the mordant you have chosen into 1 cup of water. Add this mixture to a large pot containing at least 1 gallon of water. Use the above measures of mordant for each 8 ounces of fiber. Add the fabric, making sure there is enough water to cover, and simmer for 1 to 4 hours, depending on the color intensity that you want to achieve. Turn off the heat and let the fabric rest for another 4 hours; rinse, and dry.*

*There are many other flowers and leafy materials that you can boil for color. Experiment with flowers you have on hand; interesting little rocks, berries, twigs, and even insects all yield pretty colors. Just be careful working with plant materials that are unfamiliar to you—make sure no child or pet tries to eat or drink the materials.*

**Yield:**   1 cup of each color

# Fancy and Fast
# Dried-flower Wreaths

*The beauty of real dried flowers can be enjoyed year round, each and every year. You can gather most of the raw materials for your dried-flower arrangements from the fields and roadsides near your home, or you can purchase many of the materials from the florist shop or craft store.*

*However, it's very rewarding to find your own treasures as you garden or take your daily walk, because what you gather up for yourself will likely be unique and special to your family.*

*You will save the most money, of course, if you make everything from scratch, and you can easily decorate your house with as many wreaths as you like. In addition, even silica gel, the most expensive of the recommended drying agents, can be used over and over again, as can the corn meal or kitty litter. And by microwaving all the various pods, berries, sprays, and vines, you're getting rid of any little vermin or mold spores that might otherwise relocate from the wild to your doorstep when you bring your natural treasures home.*

*You can be as inventive or as practical as you like when making your own wreaths. For example, you can gather your own grapevines and willow branches and weave them into circles, or you can purchase ready-made wreath bases of straw, styrofoam, or grapevine; you can grow and dry your own materials in your garden for year-round enjoyment, or you can purchase just about any type of natural material from the garden supply store or florist.*

## *Drying agents*

**Silica gel, corn meal,**
*or*
**Kitty litter**

## *Generous quantity of materials for drying*

**Pods, pinecones, statice, strawflowers,
baby's breath, berries, twigs, moss
Purchased wreath form**
*or*
**A quantity of grapevine, honeysuckle,**
*or*
**Other flexible vines or branches**

## *Trimming material*

**Ribbon, lace, yarn, silk flowers,**
*or*
**Tiny birds and other figurines
Florist's wire, florist's picks, pipe cleaners,
long twist-ties, string, florist's tape
Wire clippers
Scissors
White glue
Hot glue gun (optional)**

1   Dry the natural treasures you gather by any one of the
following methods: either place the material in a single layer
on absorbent paper toweling and microwave on low to medium power for anywhere from 2 to 10 minutes, depending
on the thickness and the quantity of materials; or place
materials on 1 cup of cornmeal, kitty litter, or silica gel

spread in a shallow glass microwave tray and warm for 10 to 20 minutes on medium power. Check material every 5 minutes for dampness or brittleness.

2   Gather and store your dried materials so that you have easy access to them when you begin to assemble your wreath. Plastic shoe boxes let you see what you have, or try arranging your materials, by size, in clean, cut-off paper milk cartons.

3   Prepare your pods, flowers, and pinecones by twisting florist's wire or specially prepared florist's picks around the base of the material, leaving a tail to attach to the wreath. Wrap exposed ends with green or brown florist's tape or use pipe cleaners in colors to match the materials.

4   If you are making your own wreath bases from vines, you should plan on either soaking the vines overnight in a basin of warm water to soften before you weave them or softening them one by one by microwaving them on low or medium/low power for 90 seconds to 2 minutes in just enough water to cover. Microwaving them is easier if you're working with only a few vines and you want to get started right away. You can also weave them as you cut them, before they dry out—I've had good luck with just cutting, wrapping with wire, and weaving the vines as I walk along—and the finished circles are easier to carry than a grocery bag full of vines.

5   If you are going to attach ribbon in long loops or weave a dried-seed vine in with the base wreath, arrange these materials around the base before attaching the smaller, individual items. Attach the long ribbon loops at strategic points to the base with white paste or spots of glue from the glue gun.

6   Try to visualize what the major accents for your wreath will be before you begin to attach your ornaments or flowers, because it is much easier to attach than detach. Place the

biggest items where you want them and attach with florist's picks, glue, and wire. Finish your design with various small items until the wreath looks balanced and pretty.

7   Once you are satisfied with the look of your wreath, use a pipe cleaner for a hanging loop and attach it at the back of the wreath by looping it through and twisting off the ends. Test the hanging loop before trusting it to your door to make sure it is secure. Use two loops if your wreath is particularly heavy.

**Hint:**

*As you go about gathering your materials for drying, save a few fresh flowers for pressing. Place them on paper toweling, then between layers of newspaper, then weight with books. Use your pressed flowers to decorate some of the plainer jars you've saved—simply glue the flowers with a small amount of white glue and fill the jars with your creams from Chapter 1.*

**Yield:**   1 wreath

# Microwave Potpourri

*A potpourri is a perfect gift for any time of the year. It is a mixture of spices, blossoms, herbs, and scented oils that you dry, either naturally or in the microwave, and then mix up, let mellow, and enjoy throughout the year. If you gather and dry your own ingredients, you can be most generous with it, and that's how it's meant to be used. Try mounding the delightful mixture in open bowls, big pearly seashells, or pretty glass jars. Or, try sewing a bit of the potpourri into small sachets that you tuck into drawers, closets, or suitcases.*

*You can mix up the different spices and let them blend and cure on their own, or you can jumpstart the process by microwaving them on low power for 2 to 3 minutes to speed up the process. I like the microwave process, myself, because it helps dry the ingredients a little faster, thus ensuring against mold and mildew, which can easily ruin a large amount of material if you are not vigilant during the drying process. Plus, when you're putting together gifts in a hurry, you can use all the time you save.*

*The following mixtures impart different scents—some spicy, some flowery—all wonderful.*

## Spicy Mixture

2 tablespoons allspice
2 tablespoons cinnamon
2 tablespoons nutmeg
2 tablespoons whole cloves
2 tablespoons dried citrus: lemon, orange, or lime peel
2 tablespoons borax
10 drops essential oil or perfume
2 teaspoons orrisroot

1   Combine all ingredients except oil and orrisroot and microwave in small portions on low to medium power for 2 minutes per mixture. Check for dryness after 24 hours.

2   Combine the separate dried portions and add the oil and orrisroot. Store in a glass jar, tightly covered, and let potpourri sit for 5 to 6 weeks. Turn jar once a day.

*Yield:*  7 ounces

# Springtime Mixture

**2 quarts rose petals**
**1 quart geranium petals**
**1 cup peppermint leaves**
**1 cup lavender petals**
**8 whole cloves**
**1 tablespoon ground nutmeg**
**10 drops rose oil**
**2 teaspoons orrisroot**

1   To dry flower petals, pick them in the morning right after the dew has dried. Layer petals on a tray in microwave and dry on low setting for 4 minutes. Repeat 4-minute cycles until the individual petals are brittle to the touch. Cool before using.

2   Combine all ingredients and store in a glass jar, tightly covered, and let the potpourri sit for 5 to 6 weeks. Turn the jar once a day.

*Yield:*  60 ounces

# Moth-Scat Mixture

**1/2 cup fresh lavender petals**
**1/2 cup cedar shavings**
**2 tablespoons dried thyme**
**1/4 cup fresh thyme**
**2 tablespoons dried rosemary**
*or*
**1/4 cup fresh rosemary**
**2 tablespoons cloves**
**1 tablespoon caraway seeds**
**1 tablespoon mace**
**1 tablespoon cinnamon**
**1 tablespoon nutmeg**
**1 tablespoon black pepper**
**1 teaspoon orrisroot**

1    Layer petals on a tray in microwave and dry on low setting for 4 minutes. Repeat 4-minute cycles until the individual petals are brittle to the touch. Cool before using.

2    Combine all ingredients and store in a glass jar, tightly covered, and let the potpourri sit for 5 to 6 weeks. Turn the jar once a day.

*Ideas:*
*Pretty bowls and big seashells are ideal containers for potpourri.*

*Make simple little sachets by cutting circles of fabric, placing a teaspoon of potpourri in the middle, and closing with ribbon. Place in drawers or on shelves between linens.*

*Fancy lace handkerchiefs make easy sachets, tied and used as above.*

*Yield:*   14 ounces

# 5

# Quick and Qwacky Crafts for Children

*All the following play and craft items should be created first by a parent or older child and then used for supervised play with the young child. Use the playtime to teach your child about microwave safety as well as to brush up and learn new craft skills. Although many creative and bright children can be encouraged to help in the preparation of their toys, they should not be allowed to play unsupervised with the microwave until you're sure of their maturity.*

## *Recipes and Instructions*

# Microwave Papier-mâché

*Here is a recipe for a paper-mush sculpture material that is cheap and durable, yet easy for an older child to mix up and work with. If you use shredded newspaper in this recipe, make sure that the newspaper ink won't be a problem—wear rubber gloves if you want to keep your hands clean, and plan on painting the finished product if you don't want a gray-colored creation.*

*This recipe creates a heavy mush that must soak for 24 hours before using, so plan ahead if you would like to use the mixture for masks, holiday favors, or special gifts.*

*Suggestions follow the main recipe for additional things to make with the basic mâché, or with a version that uses long strips of paper dipped into paste, with a finer mixture.*

**6 cups shredded newspaper, paper towels,**
*or*
**Other soft, absorbent paper**
**Large pot**
**Boiling water**
**Cheesecloth or porous fabric (optional)**

## *Paste*

**1 cup flour**
**3/4 cup water**

**Sturdy, gallon-size plastic bags**

1   Make sure the newspaper is ripped into very small pieces—1-inch squares are not too small. Put the shredded paper into a large pot and microwave a bowl of water on high power for 4 minutes and remove when boiling. Pour enough boiling water over the paper to cover it. Stir the paper around with a big wooden spoon or stick to make sure that all the paper is completely saturated with the water. Let this mixture steep uncovered, outside the microwave, for 24 hours.

2   Scoop out the paper mush and place a few handfuls of it onto the cheesecloth. Squeeze, press, and wring as much water as possible out of it. You can also squeeze the water out by placing a small amount of the mush in the palm of your hand and squeezing, but the cloth method is more efficient.

3   Make a quantity of paste to mix in with the paper mush by slowly adding the water to the flour, stirring constantly.

4   Measure out 1 cup of the squeezed-out mush and place it in a sturdy plastic bag with 1/3 cup of the flour paste. Knead and squeeze the materials in the bag until they are thoroughly mixed. If there is room in the bag, add another cup of mush and 1/3 cup of paste. Repeat the process with extra plastic bags until all the paper mush is combined with paste. Knead until smooth; label and keep the mixture stored in the bag in the refrigerator for up to one month.

### How to Use:

*There are many creative, inexpensive ways to use papier-mâché. One of the most basic procedures begins with making a form or an armature out of chicken wire, bent wire coat hangers, hollow paper tubes, masking tape, and just about any kind of rigid form that you can spare—it will disappear forever under layers and layers of the mush. Once you've constructed the skeleton of your intended figure, you will carefully layer the papier-mâché on top of the form, little by little, building up features, rounding out limbs, making lumps and mounds. Let dry completely and then paint.*

***Yield:*** 28 ounces papier-mâché

# Halloween Masks

*Use another version of the basic papier-mâché to form very interesting masks at Halloween. This procedure will require an extra batch of the flour and water paste, as well as a supply of newspaper strips that are 1 inch wide.*

*Begin by blowing up a sturdy balloon. Tape on a wad of crumpled newspaper for the nose, and then use the basic mixture to build up the special features for an interesting face. Two noses might make a creature from another world. Always remember to make eye holes to peer through and a breathing hole somewhere in the front.*

*Then dip the strips into the paste and carefully lay them on top of the bumps and criss-cross them all over the balloon until the balloon is completely covered (leaving a hole at the bottom for your neck). Once your Halloween face has dried, you merely pop the balloon and you can place the big mask over your head.*

*Or, you could try oiling a big beach ball with petroleum jelly or salad oil and then build the face. In the beach-ball method, remember to work only halfway around the ball. when the mask is completely dry, carefully peel it away from the ball and try it on.*

# Jack-o'-Lantern Candy Holder

*While your child is busy making a mask for Halloween, you can follow the same procedure and make a permanent Jack-o'-Lantern to hold candy and treats at the front door. Use the balloon method with either the papier-mâché mush or strips, and remember to carve out the vertical pumpkin ridges along the sides and back.*

# Mexican Party Piñata

*Another good idea for papier-mâché is to make a piñata for a child's party. Again, form your basic shape around a balloon, but this time, leave an opening in the top large enough to drop in the candies and favors. Then, once your treasures are inside, seal it up with more papier-mâché and paint or decorate with crepe paper.*

# Model Railroad Scenery

*If your child is interested in model railroads, you can make tunnels and all sorts of elevated landscape scenes from papier-mâché. Make a tunnel by stapling chicken wire to a sturdy board and then adding the papier-mâché. Finish your miniature landscapes with coffee grounds for dirt, ground herbs and moss for grass and bushes, and sawdust for sand.*

# Relief Maps of Your Neighborhood

*Using the same principles, you can make relief maps of your neighborhood for a geography project by first studying a contour map of the area and then building up hills and elevations where indicated.*

# Puppet Stage Background Scenery

*You can make very interesting background scenery for a puppet show theater or stage play by first creating flats from sturdy cardboard or plywood and then building up the protruding features of your scenery with an armature of chicken wire or wads of newspaper taped to the flat. Make sure to secure the papier-mâché you add by stapling.*

### Ideas:

*For a finer working medium, use a special mixture of papier-mâché made exclusively from tissue or toilet paper and paste to add special details to your regular creations.*

*For an unusual finishing touch to a mask or piñata, try pressing leaves and feathers in overlapping patterns into the mixture while it is still wet.*

# Sand Sculpture

*Here is a special modeling compound for the older child to tackle. With it, you can make permanent castles and sand dunes—and you can even have some fun at the preparation stage. Because sand holds heat very well, it is perfectly safe to plunge your hands into the mixture while it is still bubbling hot from the oven. The sand will feel warm to the touch, rather than hot, but you may find that the mixture is too rough for little fingers to mold with.*

**2 cups clean sand**
**1 cup water**
**1 cup cornstarch**

1   Mix together the sand, water, and cornstarch and microwave in a glass bowl on low/medium for 5 minutes. Stir and repeat at 5-minute intervals until mixture thickens. This process may take two or three microwave cycles.

2   Turn the thickened sand mixture out onto a cookie sheet or into a shallow cardboard box. Work with it immediately. It will stiffen as it cools.

3   Dry finished pieces in microwave on low power for 1 hour. Remove from oven and let pieces finish drying for another 4 hours.

4   Finish by sanding rough edges with an emery board. Add fancy details such as flags, house trim, moss, bushes, etc., either while still warm and pliable or when dried, with white glue.

**Yield:**   22 ounces

# Children's Play Dough

*There are many different kinds of dough or baker's clay to work with. This version is best for young children because it stays soft and pliable, and if you organize the ingredients and measures, even the smallest children can help to mix up and color their own batches.*

**2 cups flour
1 cup salt
1/2 cup water
1 teaspoon vinegar
Food coloring or Nature's Colors (page 90)
1/4 teaspoon peppermint extract**

1   In a large bowl, mix the flour and salt. There is no need to sift the flour first—just spoon it into a measure.

2   Slowly add the water and vinegar, microwave on low power for 1 minute, remove, and stir with a wooden spoon until the mixture is stiff. Then pick it up and knead it until pliable. If you have a young helper, break off a small piece and let the child mix and knead until the dough is soft and workable.

3   Divide the dough into separate pieces for each color desired. Poke your finger or the end of the wooden spoon into the center of each section of dough, add several drops of food coloring and peppermint extract, and knead until the color is uniform and the dough is smooth.

4   Store, tightly covered and labeled, in a plastic bag or container in the refrigerator. Play dough will keep for months if you return it to the refrigerator after each use.

### How to Use:

Take dough out of the refrigerator about 5 minutes before you're ready to play so that it will be soft enough to work easily. As long as you don't leave objects out in the air for more than a few hours, all the bits and pieces of the dough can be recombined and used over and over again.

Remember to keep similar colors together when you re-mix used pieces of dough or you will end up with nothing but dark purple-brown and dark gray pieces of clay.

On the other hand, if you like something your child has just created, you can leave it to air-dry for 24 hours or help it along by placing it in the microwave on low to medium power for 10-minute intervals. It should harden enough to paint, shellac, or spray with art fixative as described in the recipes for **Instant Crafty Clay**, page 84, and **Microwave Molding Dough**, page 86.

### Ideas:

A good way to store this **Play Dough** is to squeeze it into the skinny cans used for potato chips and then slice out small portions for each playtime.

See the recipes for **Instant Crafty Clay** and **Microwave Molding Dough** in Chapter 4 for additional ideas.

**Yield:**   22 ounces

# Fun Finger Paints

*After you whip up some finger paints for your children's pleasure, why not sit down with them and finger-paint along? I was once at a high-priced therapy session for harried middle-management types and one of the "therapies" they insisted on was for all the executives to get their hands wet with the pretty colors and "express" themselves.*

*Needless to say, this homemade therapy is certainly cheaper than the executive version, and if you sit and paint along with your kids, it's the best remedy in the world for stress. It's a good idea to store these paints in tightly closed containers if you plan to use them again. Margarine tubs are a good choice.*

**1 envelope unflavored gelatin**
**1/2 cup cornstarch**
**3 tablespoons sugar**
**2 cups cold water**
**Food coloring, Nature's Colors (page 90),**
***or***
**Tempera (powdered or liquid)**
**Dishwashing liquid detergent**
***or***
**Basic Supersaver Soft Soap (page 54)**
**White shelf paper**

1   Warm 1/4 cup water in a glass measuring cup in the microwave by cooking on medium power for 3 minutes. Soak gelatin in water for 10 minutes and put aside.

2   In a medium-size bowl, combine cornstarch and sugar, gradually add the remaining 1 3/4 cups water, and microwave on low power for 3 minutes, stir, and microwave on low for 3 more minutes or until well blended.

3   Remove from oven and add the softened gelatin. Divide mixture into separate containers for each color.

4   For each color, first add a drop or two of liquid detergent or soft soap and then the coloring, drop by drop, until you've achieved a shade you like. Food coloring is best for this, but check the various recipes in **Nature's Colors** (page 90) for other coloring ideas.

5   Store paint in the refrigerator for up to 6 weeks.

### How to Use:
*Allow children (or tense adults) plenty of paper to draw on. The glossy side of freezer wrap is good, as is plain white shelf paper. Spread the paper out onto a hard, durable, waterproof surface. Formica is excellent.*

*Have clean water and small sponges handy and begin by wetting the paper, running the dampened sponge from the middle of the paper out to the edges a few times until the paper is totally wet. Keep it wet as you work, and only let it dry when you are sure you are finished.*

### Ideas:
*If you would like to make sure the paints remain usuable for a long time in storage, add a few drops of glycerin to the mixture when you add the liquid detergent.*

*If your children love to work with finger paints, you can encourage their creativity by designing a wall mural from their creations. Use a whole roll of white shelf paper for this project and measure along the wall where you intend to hang the mural. Cut the shelf paper into long, equal-size lengths, spread paper and paints out on a newspaper-covered floor, and let your artists plan and execute their work on a grand scale.*

**Yield:**   20 ounces

# Flour and Water Paste

*This paste is a good choice for the younger child, because the taste is terrible, but nontoxic. This paste is good and sticky and will last for months if you keep it, safely labeled, in the refrigerator.*

**1/2 cup flour**
**3/4 cup cold water**
**3 cups water**

1   Slowly pour the cold water into flour and stir to make a paste. Next, boil the 3 cups of water in microwave on high power for 3 minutes.

2   Pour paste into the boiling water, stirring constantly. Microwave on medium for 2 minutes or until the paste is thick and smooth.

3   When cool, pour into a plastic squeeze-top container; label.

**Yield:**   28 ounces

# Glooey Glue

*This is the old school standby, a thick, white paste—nice and sticky—that is totally safe for children to make and use. The glue is ideal for all types of kiddie arts and crafts, especially paper construction and scrapbook projects.*

**3 tablespoons cornstarch**
**4 tablespoons cold water**
**2 cups water**

1    Microwave the 2 cups water in a glass bowl on high power for 3 minutes or until it reaches a vigorous boil. While microwaving, mix the cornstarch and cold water in a small bowl. Remove the boiling water from the oven, and pour the paste into it, stirring constantly. Microwave gently on low power for 1 or 2 minutes to thicken.

2    When liquid is clear and thick, remove from oven and let cool. Pour into a plastic squeeze container and label.

*Yield:*   19 ounces

# Birdy Gourds

*Almost any variety of gourd can be transformed into an interesting birdy for a centerpiece at a party or for just admiring. These birdies won't last forever, unless you poke thin holes into the gourds first, let them dry out, and then coat them with clear fixative when you are done.*

**Gourds**
**Acrylic paint**
**Movable animal eyes**
**Toothpicks**
**Construction paper**
**Thin wire or pieces of coat-hanger wire**
**White glue**
**Small piece of cork, bark, or stone**

1   Choose an interesting-looking gourd. Study its color and shape to determine just what kind of bird it might become. Then paint on appropriate features, quick-dry in microwave on low power for 2 minutes, glue on two movable eyes, and add either a toothpick or little half-circle of construction paper for a beak.

2   Dip two pieces of wire or two toothpicks into the glue and then into the bottom of the bird for legs. Bend the bottom of the wire and glue the bird onto a rock, or press the legs into cork or bark. You might add a bit of moss to the rock or cork and a little string worm to the beak for special effects.

*Yield:*   1 birdy gourd

# Gourd Bird Feeder and Nest

*Make a pleasant and pretty home for the birds by using available materials—you can even fit the gourds out with nesting materials or customize your nests for a purple martin apartment house.*

**1 gourd**
**1/2 cup bird food**
**Straw, soft lint, strings, or thread**
**Wire for hanging**
**White glue**
**Wooden dowel or pencil**
**Wire clippers**
**Sharp knife**

1   With a sharp knife, carve out a circle on the front of the gourd and scoop out all the insides. Discard the pulp. Microwave on low power for 15 minutes to start the drying process, check for dryness, and continue on low for another 15 minutes, if necessary. Let the gourd stand at room temperature overnight.

2   If you are making a feeder, make a hole for the wooden dowel or pencil just below the larger opening. Pierce the gourd where the dowel or pencil perch will go, glue one end of the dowel or pencil, and stick into the smaller hole. Let perch dry thoroughly.

3   Fill the gourd with the bird food if you are making a feeder or with the nesting materials if you are making a nest. Hang with the wire from a branch.

*Yield:*   1 bird feeder or nest

# New Age Rock Candy Crystals

*Here is a project and a treat for one of those days when your children have had their share of natural foods; this frankly sweet treat can at least be undertaken as an easy chemistry lesson. You'll find this a fun way to explain the magic of crystals to your children and, in this case, you will be also be able to eat the crystals that form.*

**4 cups sugar**
**1 cup water**
**Food coloring or Nature's Colors (page 90)**
**Clean glass jar**
**String, cut into 6-inch lengths**
**Pencil**

1   Dissolve 2 cups of sugar in 1 cup of water by microwaving on high power for 4 minutes; remove and stir. If all the sugar has not dissolved, repeat cycle. Remove the solution carefully because the container and water will be superhot. Gradually add a few drops of the food coloring of your choice and the remaining sugar, stirring continuously until all the sugar is dissolved.

2   Pour the solution into a clean glass jar. Tie the pieces of string to the pencil and suspend them across the mouth of the jar so that the ends hang into the sugar water.

3   Crystals suitable to eat will form in an hour and continue for several days to a week. Pieces can be broken off and eaten after the first hour.

*Yield:*   12 ounces

# Soap Crayons

*Here's one way to lure any child into the bathtub—even the most dyed-in-the-wool-scaredy-cat. These crayons are fun to make, fun to use, and they can make bathtub cleaning a lot easier if you teach your child to circle the ring around the tub and scrub it away. Let bubbling artists paint the sides of the tub, the tile walls around the tub, and then let them create self-portraits by coloring all over their bodies with these nontoxic crayons. Then just wash everything down and do it again tomorrow.*

**1 cup soap flakes**
**1/4 cup hot water**
**Food coloring or Nature's Colors (page 90)**

1   Have ready one large bowl and several small bowls, one for each color. You will also need an ice cube tray with a section divider or separate containers to act as small molds. The segmented plastic dividers used to pack ravioli or fancy cookies will also work, but first test the mold by microwaving for 1 minute on low power to be sure the lighter plastic will not crumple in the microwave.

2   Put soap flakes in a large bowl and warm the water in a glass measuring cup in the microwave by heating on medium power for 2 minutes. Keep water and the measuring cup warm and drop the water into the soap flakes, a teaspoonful at a time, stirring constantly. The mixture will be extremely thick and hard to stir.

3   Spoon some of the soap into each of the small bowls and color each separately, adding the color by drops until the soap has the consistency of a very thick paste.

4   Gently press spoonfuls of the paste into your molds and microwave on low for 15 minutes to dry them out. Remove and set the crayons aside at room temperature for a few hours to harden. However, don't be surprised if they take a couple of days to harden completely. (The harder they are, the longer they will last in water.)

5   When dry, remove crayons from the molds and allow to set for an  additional day before using.

### Note:
*If these crayons will be used by very small children who might put them into their mouths, use only the natural dyes in* **Nature's Colors** *on page 90. Otherwise, it is safe to use regular food coloring from the kitchen.*

**Yield:**   20 crayons

# Bag-its

*Here's a way to microwave up soft and cuddly bean bags that give a satisfying thunk when tossed around by little children and even younger grown-ups. You should try to personalize them—make cute and huggable ones for one kind of child, make smart and silly bean bags for another kind of child, and then make a fun target to toss them into.*

*Just remember to keep in mind the size of the hand that the bean bags are meant for: don't make them too big and heavy for a tiny child.*

**1 pound navy or pinto beans**
**1 yard colorful, closely woven fabric, such as:**
**cotton, terry cloth, corduroy, felt, or gabardine**

1    Spread beans in a flat or very shallow microwave baking pan and bake on low power for 20 minutes to kill any vermin and to prevent beans from sprouting. Let beans cool completely before using.

2    Fold your fabric in half lengthwise, with right sides together. Create a simple pattern from an illustration in a child's coloring book or create a pattern of your own design; cut two pieces for each bean bag. With right sides together, sew twice around the design leaving a 1/2-inch margin. Use a small, tight machine stitch or, if sewing by hand, a sturdy lock stitch. Leave a 2-inch opening for pouring in the beans.

3    Turn the bag right side out and press with a warm iron. If you are creating an animal or imaginary character, add the features and details. Feel free to improvise and add your own ideas, especially if you are letting a child help with this project. Just make certain that you don't add any details or small elements that can be chewed off by a very small child,

and don't sew on any plastic or hard-edged trinkets that may hurt someone if the bean bag is thrown astray.

4   Fill the bean bag with the cooled beans until the bag is 1 to 2 inches thick and still soft and flexible. Sew up the hole left for the beans.

### Variations:

Create a simple target-toss game by making small round bean bags and decorating an oatmeal box or a small carton for the target, if desired.

Or, if you really feel that you have no sewing talents at all, pour the beans loosely into a small, woolen mitten or glove, sew up the opening, and decorate as you see fit. Your kids will never know the difference and they will still appreciate their bean bag toy because they know it's made with love— even if it's not a work of art.

**Yield:**   4 to 6 bean bags, depending on size

# Secret Picture Puzzles

*To make a special birthday party invitation, try sending a jigsaw puzzle—the pieces stuffed into an envelope look truly mysterious until you follow the clues for reassembling. For an added puzzle within a puzzle, write a secret message on the cardboard before you make it into a jigsaw and include instructions for "decoding" the secret.*

*A variation on the puzzle theme is to select one of your child's favorite photos and have it enlarged, giving you the base for another very special puzzle. Other types of pictures, cut from magazines, can also be used for an interesting, custom puzzle. In each case, remember the age and skill of the child who will be solving the jigsaw as you determine the size and difficulty of the puzzle pieces.*

**White glue or Gooey Glue (page 114)**
**8-inch-by-10-inch photo, magazine illustration,**
***or***
**Drawing**
**Shirt cardboard or bristol board**
**Acrylic fixative (optional)**
**Sharp scissors or X-Acto knife**
**1/2 cup lemon juice**
**Cotton swab or clean fountain pen**

1    Glue the picture or drawing of your choice onto the cardboard. If you plan to make an invitation, a letter, or a special message your puzzle base, you can write directly on the cardboard with the cotton swab or fountain pen dipped in the lemon juice. If the cardboard is too dark, write your message on clean white paper and paste it to the reverse side of the cardboard.

2   Spray or brush the photo or picture with acrylic fixative if you expect it to have heavy use, but do not spray acrylic fixative on the lemon-juice side.

3   Draw puzzle shapes directly onto the cardboard to suit the skill of your child. Keep the pieces large and easy to handle, as well as simple to cut out, if a small child will work on the puzzle.

4   Carefully cut around the shapes you've drawn with a pair of small, sharp scissors or an X-Acto knife.

### How to Use:

*To solve the mystery of the secret puzzle, add instructions to hold each piece up to a light bulb until the secret lemon-juice writing appears.*

*For an especially puzzling puzzle, try writing your message in only a small portion of the entire puzzle, leaving the rest of the pieces blank.*

**Yield:**   1 to 10 puzzles

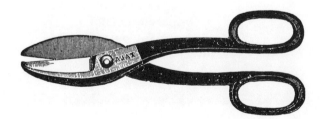

# Instant Sweatshirts

*These are the ultimate designer sweatshirts, and they are ready in only a few minutes because you dry them as you create them in your microwave oven. Once you've gotten the hang of this, you can invent your own methods of painting, drying, gluing, and stenciling. To start you off with a guaranteed success, here are a few techniques for creating some truly individual, one-of-a-kind garments for your child. The ideas for decorating sweatshirts that are described here can also be used for other items—jeans, jackets, knapsacks, even doll clothes.*

*However, these projects are messy and the results aren't always predictable, so it's a good idea to start with something simple and not too expensive, until you get the knack of painting and decorating.*

**Sweatshirt or other garment**
**Opaque acrylic paints**
**White glue**
**1/2 cup sand**
**Buttons, snaps, fringe, assorted trimmings**
**Paper doilies**
**Popsicle sticks**
**Sponge or fat paintbrush**
**Crocheted lace with large loops**
**Newspapers**

# Dribble Painting

1   Spread the newspapers out on the work surface and place the sweatshirt, carefully spread out, on the newspapers. Choose the colors of acrylic paint that you wish to dribble across the garment and dip a popsicle stick into the paint. Gently wave it over the sweatshirt, letting small drops and long streamers of paint fall in a random pattern.

2   For special effects, try mixing a small batch of textured paint by squeezing a teaspoon of white glue into a sandwich bag and adding a few drops of paint and a tablespoon of sand. Squish the bag around a bit and then cut a tiny hole in the corner. Squeeze your textured paint on in a swirly pattern.

3   You can always allow the garment to dry for 24 hours before wearing, but you can speed up the procces when kids can't wait by microwaving newly painted and decorated garments on low power for 15- to 30-minute cycles. Check the garments during the process to make sure that they don't burn or scorch and that the acrylics don't melt.

4   Buttons, trim, fringe, and snaps can also be added if desired after the drying is finished.

# Doily Stencil

1   Cut a paper doily in half and arrange the two pieces on the shoulders of the sweatshirt. Another full doily can be added to the front and back of the sweatshirt, if desired.

2   Dip a sponge or fat paintbrush into the acrylic paint and gently sponge or brush it over the doily. Remove the doily and dry as described above before wearing.

# Charm Sweatshirt

*If your child collects plastic charms, this sweatshirt idea will allow her to show them off.*

After your sweatshirt has been painted or decorated with paint, sew lace trim along the front of the sweatshirt, stitching along the seam allowance of the lace. Attach the charms to the loops in the edging.

**Hint:**
*To set the acrylic paints on a stencil or dribble design, mix a solution of:*

**1/2 cup vinegar**
**1/2 cup water**

*Fold the painted items with the paint side out. Place on several layers of absorbent toweling. Dip a clean dish towel or washcloth into the solution and press it directly onto the painted areas. Warm the garment in the microwave for 10 minutes on medium to low power, or until completely dry.*

**Yield:**   1 decorated sweatshirt

# Mush-melt Wrapping Paper

*These wraps are especially colorful and suited to kids' art and kids' tastes. No grandparent will be able to tear into these without first complimenting the child—it's almost like presenting two presents at once. Stay close at hand to supervise this project, even for older children, because the mess is supposed to be made on the wrapping paper, not in the surrounding kitchen.*

**Newspaper**
**Absorbent paper**
**Vegetable peeler or penknife**
**Bits and pieces of broken crayons**
**Oven mitts or old gloves**

1   Cover microwave surface with several layers of absorbent toweling and lay the sheet of paper you will use for wrapping paper on top of the towel. With the vegetable peeler or penknife, whittle off shavings of different colors of crayon until the surface is covered.

2   Microwave on medium to high power for 2 to 10 minutes, or until the shavings begin to melt.

3   Make sure your child wears gloves, either two oven mitts or old winter gloves, for this next step. Remove the paper from the oven, fold in half or into quarters, and have your child press his or her hands all over the paper to mush the melted crayon into pretty designs. Unfold the paper immediately and let it cool.

*Yield:*   2 to 10 sheets of custom wrapping paper

# Nature's Dolls

*Archaeologists have found evidence that dolls were among the earliest toys ever invented. Even cliff dwellers and cave people made dolls for their young ones to hold. All societies have dolls. They can be fashioned out of anything on hand—twigs, grasses, bits of cloth. Some of the most charming are the simple ones that allow the child to add special features and details. The following doll ideas are classic ones, and you will probably devise more after you begin with these.*

## Corn-husk Doll

*For a rough, simple doll, you can use corn husks just as you take them from the corn, moistened and microwaved to make them pliable. For fancier dolls, you can bleach, soften, and tint the corn husks in delicate colors to suggest skirts, shawls, and hats.*

**Corn husks**
**2 cups water**
**2 tablespoons bleach**
**Paper towels**
**Nature's Colors (page 90) or fabric dye (optional)**
**Cotton ball, wooden bead, or small styrofoam ball**
**Twist ties or thin wire**
**Corn silk**
**White glue**
**Felt-tip markers**

1   If you want to make a fancy doll, first place the corn husks in a pan of water to which 2 tablespoons of bleach have been added. Let soak for 2 hours and then microwave

for 10 minutes on low. Remove, rinse, and let drain on absorbent paper toweling.

2   To tint corn husks, dip into the dye of your choice and let the husks remain until a desirable color tint is achieved. To speed up the dyeing process or to increase the color tones more quickly, microwave the corn husks in the dipping mixture on low to medium power for 5 minutes, check the color, and repeat cycle if necessary. Remove, blot on paper toweling, and keep moist and pliable by storing in a plastic bag in the refrigerator until needed.

3   To make a doll, fold several long strips of husk lengthwise over a cotton ball, bead, or styrofoam ball to make a head. Tie at the neck with a thin strip of husk, wire, or a twist tie.

4   Right beneath the neck, weave a few husks horizontally through the lengthwise husks. These husks will form the arms. Tie off the ends and puff out the arms to suggest full sleeves.

5   Tie off a waist by binding the lengthwise cornhusks below the arms, and shape the bottom of the husks into two pantaloons, if desired. Otherwise, let the husks remain gathered in a skirt.

6   Braid some of the corn silk and glue it on the head. Cut a triangle of corn husk as a kerchief or a cap, and another for a shawl, if desired.

7   Add facial features with felt-tip marker.

*Yield:*   1 doll

# Hollyhock Doll

*This is a simple little doll that will charm a child with its delicate, transitory beauty.*

**1 large, open hollyhock blossom**
**1 leaf**
**Several toothpicks**
**1 seed case, closed**
**1 seed case, with calyx**
**Tiny twigs**
**1 cup drying material: silica gel, corn meal,**
*or*
**Kitty litter**

1   Arange all the natural materials on a shallow tray or absorbent toweling in the microwave and warm on low power for 90 seconds. Materials should remain pliable. Use the large, open hollyhock, held upside down, to form the skirt. Fasten a leaf over the skirt with a length of broken toothpick to form a simple apron.

2   A closed seed case makes the upper torso, and a seed case with calyx intact will form the head. Attach one on top of the other with toothpicks.

3   Attach tiny twigs to the sides of the middle seed case for arms.

4   Pour the drying material into a shallow glass bowl or pan and carefully stand the finished doll upright in the drying material. Microwave on medium power for 10 to 15 minutes, checking every 5 minutes for moisture. The finished doll will be smaller and more wizened than the fresh version, but it will last for a season or two.

*Yield:*   1 doll

# Zippy Snacks
# and
# Spices

*This chapter will show you how to prepare simple snacks and fruit, herb, and spice concoctions with the quick drying action that your microwave provides. Once you've prepared fresh snacks and spices this way, a variety of flavoring mixes can be made in quantity for stocking your pantry or for giving away as special, personalized gifts to friends and family, as suggested in Chapter 9. In addition, drying and preserving lets you save the leftovers from all those fresh herbs and spices you gather for your homemade soups and stews. By drying them as soon as you've used what you needed, you preserve their original freshness, taste, and zest.*

# *Recipes and Instructions*

# Chewie Cheesies

*My children have always loved cheese snacks, especially these. They are also delicious as an accompaniment to a hearty bowl of homemade soup. It's very easy to make the dough ahead of time and chill it for a few days or freeze it until needed.*

**1 cup flour**
**1 teaspoon salt**
**1/8 teaspoon paprika**
**2 cups Cheddar cheese, grated**
**1/4 cup butter**

1   Sift flour, salt, and paprika together and stir in cheese.

2   Cream butter in a food processor or with an electric mixer and slowly add the flour mixture, mixing until well blended.

3   Shape mixture into a roll, wrap in wax paper, and chill in refrigerator overnight.

4   Slice the chilled dough very thin and place on a flat microwave sheet or paper plate. Roll and twist the slices into little crescents. Microwave for 3 minutes on high power, rotate, and microwave for 2 minutes on medium. Cool until set and wrap crescents in foil or store in a tightly closed container for 1 to 2 days.

*Yield:*   24 crescents

# Homemade Bagel Chips

*Bagel chips are snappy and delicious. They're also an excellent way to use stale bagels before they turn to stone. You have to work fast and slice them up while you still can—otherwise your only recourse with old bagels is to laminate them and use them as large refrigerator magnets or small doorstops.*

**3 bagels**
**1/8 cup vegetable oil**
**1 tablespoon garlic salt**

1   Slice bagels crosswise into very thin slices and arrange on microwave tray. Using a pastry brush, lightly coat both sides of the slice with the vegetable oil and sprinkle with the garlic salt.

2   Microwave for 5 minutes on medium power, turn once, rotate, and microwave for 3 minutes more, or until both sides are crisp.

*Yield:*   16 ounces

# Snappy Croutons

*If you store these croutons in a tightly closed container in the refrigerator, you can add new ones to the batch indefinitely. Use these delicious, crunchy nuggets to enhance salads, add interest to soups and stews, as a top layer on scalloped tomatoes, or as the basis of all sorts of stuffings for turkey, chicken, and even for your own* **Mix 'n Match Stuffing Mix** *(page 137).*

**1 cup day-old bread or rolls, cubed**
**2 tablespoons butter**
**1 teaspoon seasoning: onion salt,**
**garlic salt, grated cheese, paprika, thyme,**
**poultry seasoning, or tarragon**

1   Melt butter by microwaving in a glass or microwave-safe measuring cup for 2 minutes on high power.

2   Stir the seasoning of your choice into the melted butter.

3   Toss the flavored butter with the cubed bread, making sure each piece is coated. Place in shallow microwave dish.

4   Microwave for 5 minutes, shake and rotate the dish, bake on medium power for 2 minutes, shake and rotate again, and bake on low 2 more minutes. Let stand to cool.

5   Store in a covered container in the refrigerator for up to 2 months, and replenish with the different versions of croutons described here. Shake vigorously to distribute all the different flavors before dipping a portion out of the container.

### Variations:
*Fry up 4 slices of bacon on absorbent toweling in the microwave on high power for 3 minutes or until crispy; remove*

*bacon to fresh paper towels to drain excess grease. Allow to cool and then crumble bacon and toss together with the cubes for a crunchy treat.*

*Add 1/2 cup of lightly browned chopped onions, green peppers, or celery to the cubes and then cook as directed.*

# Mexicali Croutons

1/2 cup bread, cubed
1/2 cup nacho chips, crumbled
1 tablespoon El Paso Seasonings Mix (page 148)
1 tablespoon corn oil

# Italian-flavored Croutons

1 cup bread, cubed
1/2 teaspoon oregano
1/2 teaspoon garlic powder
1/2 teaspoon basil
1 tablespoon olive oil

# Cheesy Soup Croutons

1 cup bread, cubed
1/4 cup Parmesan or Cheddar cheese, grated
1 tablespoon butter, melted

Gently toss all ingredients together in a large bowl, spread in a shallow microwave pan, microwave for 5 minutes on medium, rotate and repeat cycle, and store as directed for **Snappy Croutons**.

*Yield:* 8 ounces

# Mix 'n Match Stuffing Mix

*Here's a neat way to use up all those odds and ends of bread that seem to collect in the bread box at the end of each week. You can feed your bread to the birds, of course, but if you want to feed it to your family, you can make an instant stuffing mix that adds flavor and elegance to leftover turkey or chicken or just about any meat. This basic mix is flavored for chicken, but you can vary the spices for pork or beef.*

1/4 **cup onion, minced**
1/2 **cup celery, minced**
6 **cups bread, cubed**
1 **tablespoon parsley flakes**
3 **cubes chicken bouillon, crumbled**
*or*
3 **tablespoons chicken bouillon powder**
1 **teaspoon thyme**
1 **teaspoon pepper**
1/2 **teaspoon sage**
1/2 **teaspoon salt**

1   Spread the celery and onion in a shallow layer on a microwave tray. Blot excess moisture and dry in your microwave on medium setting in 2-minute cycles. Remove from oven and let cool while you prepare the bread.

2   Spread bread on a microwave dish and bake for 2 to 3 minutes on medium to high power, rotating twice to warm evenly. Cool.

3   In a large bowl, toss bread cubes with the rest of the seasonings until the cubes are evenly coated. Store in a tightly

closed container in the pantry for 1 to 4 months; mixture can also be kept in the freezer for up to 12 months.

### How to Use:

*Combine 2 cups **Stuffing Mix** with 1/2 cup water and 2 tablespoons melted butter. Stir to mix thoroughly, microwave on high power for 2 minutes, and stir again right before serving. You can also rewarm the stuffing in a pan on top of the stove, in the microwave oven, or in a regular oven.*

### Ideas:

*To change the flavor of the basic stuffing mix to accompany different meats, add any of the following spices and flavors to 2 cups of mix:*

## Pork Stuffing

**1/2 teaspoon sage**
**1/4 cup apple, chopped**
**1/4 cup nuts, chopped**

## Turkey Stuffing

**1/4 cup raisins**
**1/4 cup apple, chopped**
**1/4 cup cranberries, chopped**

## Beef Stuffing

**1/4 cup canned or fresh mushrooms**
**2 tablespoons Worcestershire Sauce**

**Yield:**  7 cups

# Micro Veggies

*Here is a handy way to use up celery before it becomes all limp and uncouth in the refrigerator, or to store away a nice harvest of peppers. I always buy celery, scallions, and carrots with the best of intentions, but whenever I need some in a recipe, they are usually too far gone to slice.*

*Drying a batch of vegetables in the microwave is a quick and easy way to keep them chopped and handy when you need them. They'll keep in your pantry nearly forever and will reconstitute instantly in soups and stews.*

**1 to 2 cups vegetables, finely chopped:
onions, mushrooms, red or green peppers,
scallions, celery**

1   Cover your microwave tray with paper towels and spread finely chopped vegetables in a thin layer over the paper. Blot away excess moisture before cooking.

2   Dry in microwave on low setting for 15 minutes. Rotate and microwave for another 15 minutes. Check for dryness. If necessary keep drying on low in 15-minute cycles until completely dry and crisp to the touch.

3   Cool and store immediately in a dry, sterilized glass or metal container with a tight-fitting lid. Vegetables will keep for up to 6 months in the pantry.

***Ideas:***
*You can use your microwave to dry peels from oranges, tangerines, lemons, limes, and grapefruits. Use low setting in 10-minute cycles, taking care not to scorch the skins. When they are completely dry, you can break them up for use in* **Microwave Potpourri***, page 98, or you can grind the dried peels in the blender and use them for* **Oatmeal-Citrus Scrubbing Grains***, page 16.*

To dry fresh corn, husk and clean ears of corn and steam or blanch for 3 minutes. Drain, cut kernels from the cob, and dry them the same way you dried your other vegetables. Just make sure that you use your lowest setting and check for dryness every ten minutes. When fully dry, the corn should be hard and brittle.

Pour 2 cups boiling water over 1 cup dry corn and simmer, covered, for 1 hour.

### Ideas:
Just for fun, try drying vegetables in the sun the way the early settlers did. Pick a dry sunny day and place a tray in full sunlight. Cover loosely with cheesecloth or arrange a screen above the trays. The trick is to maintain air circulation and the drying effect of the sun, and at the same time to protect the vegetables from insects and critters. Take the trays in at night and repeat the drying process for 1 to 3 days, or until vegetables are thoroughly dried.

If you do use the sun-drying method, place the food in the microwave at medium power for 5 minutes or store the food in the freezer for 24 hours before using, to kill any insect eggs which may be invisible, but nonetheless there.

## Freeze-Dried Vegetables

You can also freeze your dried vegetables. Cover with plastic wrap and freeze until firm. Store the vegetables in a freezer container or plastic bag suitable for the freezer.

### How to Use:
Use the frozen vegetables **only** for cooking. Drop them while still frozen into soups and stews, or use them for brais-ing—if you let them thaw, they will be too limp to eat.

**Yield:**  8 to 16 ounces

# "Sun" Dried Tomatoes

*If you've ever had sun-dried tomatoes from your neighborhood cucina, you know how good they can be. They are perfect served with fresh, creamy mozzarella cheese and garnished with fresh basil. Use the very best extra-virgin, first-pressed olive oil you can afford for this recipe, and save the extra oil for delicious salads.*

*Since the tomatoes must be dried carefully, it's a good idea to keep an eye on them during the drying process, because microwave drying is a lot more potent than sun-drying. We don't recommend that you try sun-drying your tomatoes because our summers are neither hot enough nor long enough to do the job as slowly and thoroughly as necessary.*

**3 pounds ripe plum tomatoes**
**2 teaspoons salt**
**1 1/2 cups olive oil**

1   Rinse tomatoes in warm water and pat dry, absorbing any remaining water with paper towels. Cut lengthwise and place, cut side up, on a microwave rack over absorbent towels or on a microwave dish. Sprinkle with salt.

2   Dry in 15-minute cycles on low power, rotating between cycles. Test for dryness and firmness between cycles. Dry for 3 hours or until tomatoes are still flexible but not moist. You will have to adjust the times given for the drying process, depending on the power of your oven. Cool.

3   Pack dried tomatoes in a sterilized glass jar, cover with olive oil, and store in a cool, dry place for 1 month before using.

**Yield:**   16 ounces

# Chewie Fruit

*This delicious way to preserve, store, and eat fruit has just recently come back into fashion. Fruit leathers are fun to pull at and to eat, and they are full of flavor. Their light weight and long chewability make them ideal to pack for hiking or for school lunches. I also make up a batch for Halloween and other snack-food holidays because they're much healthier than any candy you can get. To get the best flavors, it's a good idea to use fruit when it is at a very ripe or almost too-ripe stage.*

**2 cups fruit, fresh, frozen, cooked, or canned
1/2 cup sugar or honey**

1   Pour the fruit and sweetening into a blender container and puree until you have a very fine pulp.

2   Line a microwave sheet with plastic wrap and tape the edges securely with masking tape. Pour the puree over the plastic wrap, spreading it with a spatula so that it is a uniform thickness of about 1/8 inch.

3   Dry the puree on medium setting for 3 minutes, test it for pliability, rotate, and dry for another 2 minutes. The leather strips should be dry on the surface, but still pliable.

4   Remove the leather from the pan, keeping the plastic wrap as a backing. Cut leather and plastic into narrow strips and roll up. Store rolls in an airtight container for up to 8 weeks.

**Tip:**

   Using your microwave is a lot quicker than sun-drying, but each microwave performs differently, so the results are not entirely predictable. Therefore, test your fruit mixture frequently to make sure it doesn't overcook and crumble.

Variations:

   You can add a tablespoon of lemon juice to flavor some of the fruit puree, if you wish, and you can sprinkle the raw puree, while still spread out in the pan, with chopped nuts.

   A crushed vitamin C tablet will provide enough ascorbic acid in a peach or pear puree to keep the fruit from browning.

   For raw-apple leather, add 1/2 cup apple cider and 1/4 teaspoon cinnamon to 2 cups peeled and cored apples.

**Yield:**  16 ounces

# Salt Substitutes

*There are several ways to try to cut down on your salt intake if you have a low tolerance for heavily salted foods. Spirited combinations of herbs and spices are one way, using a salt substitute as part of a recipe is another, and the easiest way to get used to the taste of less salt is to try a substitute that leaves a little salt in, as in the following two recipes. This is also a great way to use your dried herbs and spices. You'll find that a mortar and pestle is a good way to grind the spices fine enough to sprinkle through a shaker or you can whirl the herbs and spices in a blender until you have a fine mix.*

## Mrs. Flash Mix

1/4 cup onion, finely minced
1/4 cup green pepper, finely minced
1/4 cup celery, minced
5 cloves garlic, chopped
2 tablespoons lemon peel, grated
1/4 cup parsley, finely minced
2 tablespoons dried basil
2 tablespoons salt
1 tablespoon dried oregano
1 tablespoon dried savory
1 teaspoon dried marjoram
1 teaspoon dried coriander
1 teaspoon dried cumin

**1** To dry the minced onion, green pepper, parsley, and celery, blot away any excess moisture with an absorbent towel, wrap them in another paper towel and microwave on high for 90 seconds. Check for dryness, rotate, and microwave for another 90 seconds. Repeat until dry to the touch.

**2**   Combine all ingredients and whirl in the blender until chopped fine—about 1 minute. Stop and scrape the sides of the blender often because the mixture will be a bit sticky at first. Store mixture in a tightly capped shaker jar and use in place of salt in meat and main-course recipes and on salads.

*Yield:*  14 ounces

# Sesame Salt

**1/2 cup sesame seeds**
**1 teaspoon fresh chives, chopped**
**1/4 cup sea salt**
**1 teaspoon paprika**
**1 teaspoon pepper**

1   Microwave sesame seeds and chives on high power for 2 minutes, rotate, microwave for additional 45 seconds. Let cool. Stir in salt and microwave 2 minutes more. Cool.

2   Place sesame seed mixture and the rest of the ingredients in the blender; whirl for 1 minute or until mixture is finely ground. Store in an airtight container for up to 6 months.

*Yield:*  7 ounces

# Firehouse Hot Chili Powder

*Here's a double microwave way to whip up the zestiest pot of chili east of the Pecos or north of Big Sur. The secret's in the chili powder. First, you dry your own chili peppers in the microwave. Then, you microwave all of your ingredients together before you grind them up and add them to the chili.*

*If you like your chili fiery hot, you can vary this recipe by including a bit more cayenne and using hot, rather than mild, chili peppers—but label it accordingly. This powder will have a better consistency if you use a mortar and pestle to grind the peppers and coarser spices.*

**1/2 cup mild or hot chili peppers, chopped**
**6 tablespoons paprika**
**2 tablespoons turmeric**
**1 teaspoon cumin**
**1 teaspoon dried oregano**
**1/2 teaspoon cayenne**
**1/2 teaspoon garlic powder**
**1/2 teaspoon salt**
**1/4 teaspoon ground cloves**

1   Arrange peppers in a shallow layer on a microwave tray. Blot away excess moisture with absorbent toweling. Wrap in a fresh absorbent towel and microwave on high for 90 seconds. Rotate, check for dryness, and microwave for another minute.

2   Mix all ingredients and microwave together for 2 minutes on low power in order to blend flavors. Let stand in oven for an additional minute.

3   Grind to a fine powder using a mortar and pestle, or whirl
the mixture in your food processor or blender. Spice will
keep for up to 6 months on the pantry shelf.

***How to Use:***
*This powder is somewhat more pungent and fresher
tasting than a packaged brand, so use a bit less.*

**Yield:**   8 ounces

# El Paso Seasonings Mix

*Since my family loves Mexican flavors, this seasoning mix is used constantly at our house on ground beef, mixed with cheese for topping nacho chips, and combined with sour cream for a dip. Here's the double microwave trick that will make the seasonings taste fresher than storebought: first dry your own finely chopped onion and then add it to the other ingredients. Blend and dry them thoroughly on low power to spread the flavor evenly.*

**1 Spanish or Bermuda onion, minced**
**1/3 cup beef bouillon powder**
**1/3 cup Firehouse Hot Chili Powder (page 146)**
**2 tablespoons ground cumin**
**4 teaspoons crushed red pepper**
**1 tablespoon oregano, dried**
**2 teaspoons garlic powder**

1    Spread onion in a shallow layer on a microwave tray. Blot away excess moisture and microwave on high power for 90 seconds.

2    Combine with the other ingredients and microwave on medium power for 2 minutes, or until mixture is dry. Store the mixture in an airtight container in a cool, dry pantry for up to 4 months.

*Ideas:*

*Add 1 tablespoon to recipes calling for a Mexican flavor, or sprinkle liberally on top of foods you want to spice. One tablespoon mixed with chopped tomatoes and green peppers makes a tasty dip or filling for tacos.*

*Add 1 tablespoon to shredded cheese before melting for another dip. Serve with sour cream.*

*Yield:*   16 ounces

# Curry in a Hurry

*Here is a very authentic curry powder that is much fresher tasting than the kind that has been on the store shelf for months. And since it's so easy to make, you can prepare it in small portions for extra freshness in your chicken, lamb, or beef stews.*

**1 tablespoon cumin seeds**
**1 tablespoon cardamom seeds**
**1 tablespoon coriander seeds**
**2 tablespoons ground turmeric**
**1/2 tablespoon dry mustard**
**1/2 teaspoon cayenne pepper**

1   Combine the cumin, cardamom, and coriander seeds in a glass or enamel container and microwave on low power for 5 minutes. Rotate and continue on low for another 5 minutes. Let stand in microwave for 2 minutes to cool and even out flavor.

2   Grind the seeds in the blender on high speed. Add turmeric, dry mustard, and cayenne pepper. Mix until all ingredients are well blended.

3   Store in a tightly capped container. Seasoning will keep for 1 year on the pantry shelf.

*Yield:*   3 ounces

# Celestial White Sauce Mix

*White sauce is the special touch that can make everyday dishes seem like gourmet treats, even in the middle of a hard work week. The trick is to make a perfect white sauce with no lumps in it. I realize now that it's not magic—all you have to remember is to add the liquid to the dry ingredients, stirring all the while, never the other way around, and you will have smooth, lump-free sauces.*

**2 cups instant nonfat dry milk**
**1 cup flour**
**1 teaspoon salt**
**1/2 cup vegetable shortening or butter**

1   Mix the dry ingredients and cut the shortening in with a pastry blender or two knives, or with a food processor.

2   Gently microwave in covered dish for 90 seconds on low power. Let stand for 1 minute to cool, then blend mixture with a fork.

3   Store mixture in a tightly closed container. If you are using butter, store the mix in the refrigerator; if made with vegetable shortening, the mixture will keep on the pantry shelf in dry weather for up to 6 months.

***How to Use:***
*In general, use 1/2 cup mix for every 1/2 cup liquid unless you are adding more dry ingredients, such as cheese. In that case, increase the liquid until the sauce is the consistency you like.*

***Yield:*** 27 ounces

# Don't Be Alfredo Sauce Mix

*Make a batch of* **Celestial White Sauce Mix** *using butter instead of vegetable shortening for this delicious, rich version of a classic Alfredo-type sauce. You can use fettuccine noodles for this dish—they are wide and flat and hold all the tasty sauce—and you can add cooked Italian sausage, crumbled or sliced, to the sauce before serving. Preparing this in your microwave oven is easier than preparing it on the stovetop. The sauce heats more evenly, and you don't have to worry about boil-overs.*

**1/2 cup Celestial White Sauce Mix (page 150)**
**2 to 4 cloves garlic, pressed**
**1/2 cup Parmesan or Romano cheese, grated**
**1/2 cup light cream**

1   While the pasta is cooking, assemble the ingredients and have them ready to blend and heat in your microwave. You will pour the sauce over the pasta just before serving.

2   Cook and strain the pasta and return it to the large pan used for boiling. Turn off heat.

3   Heat the Alfredo sauce mixture in a covered microwave container for 2 minutes on high. Let cool for 30 seconds to even out the flavor. Pour over pasta. Serve immediately.

*Yield:*   1 cup

# Noodle-Mania Mix

*There are lots of different mixes on the market now for spicing up and flavoring noodles, pasta, and spaghetti. But I like to make my own because it's fresher, zestier, and you can vary it each time you use it. Your kids can also learn to mix these up for slumber parties or camping trips. You'll find that this mix and its variations will save you money, time, and pantry space.*

**1 cup instant nonfat dry milk**
**2 tablespoons Romano or Parmesan cheese, grated**
**1/3 cup onion, minced**
**1 tablespoon garlic powder**
**1/2 teaspoon salt**
**1/2 teaspoon white pepper**

Combine ingredients in microwave dish, microwave on high power for 1 minute. Check for dryness, microwave for 1 minute more on high power, if necessary. Store in a tightly closed container. Mix will keep for 4 months in the pantry.

### *How to Use:*
*Combine 1/4 cup mix with 2 tablespoons melted butter and 1/4 cup milk. Toss with pasta.*

### *Idea:*
*Add 1/4 cup grated Cheddar cheese in place of the Parmesan cheese for a different taste. Or try tossing the pasta and mix with 1/2 cup braised snow peas, 1/2 cup carrot slivers, and 1/2 cup pignolia (pine) nuts for a tasty main course pasta salad.*

**Yield:**    12 ounces

# Herb Teas

*Microwaving on a low setting is an excellent way to blend the flavors of different spices and herbs. The important thing to remember is that you're neither cooking nor drying, only blending. Use this technique to create some of your very own seasoned and herb teas. If you find a blend that particularly suits you, remember that it would make a nice gift for someone else to sample. A word of caution: never try to brew a tea from an herb you can't identify. Even though a certain herb may look small and harmless, it could be dangerous and even lethal.*

*You can buy all the herbs listed in the following blends at the health food store, or, if you are patient, you can plan ahead and begin to grow some of the herbs in your annual or perennial flower beds.*

## Balmy Lemon Tea

**10 sprigs lemon thyme**
**5 sprigs lemon basil**
**5 sprigs chamomile**
**3 sprigs lemon balm**

1   Arrange herbs in a shallow layer on a microwave tray and dry at medium power in 2-minute cycles. Check for dryness, rotate tray, and repeat cycle. When properly dried, sprigs and leaves should crumble easily.

2   Blend herbs and store them in a tightly capped jar or tin.

### How to Use:

To brew tea, add 1 tablespoon of herbs to 1 cup of water. Microwave on high power for 2 minutes, remove from oven, and allow to steep for 1 minute. Lemon balm is said to reduce fevers, so you might sip this tea if you feel a fever coming on.

### Variations:

The following herbs will make a nice tea, alone or in combination. Test and find the flavors you like best.

Anise will give you a sweet licorice flavor that is supposed to be good for coughs and as an aid to sleep.

Chamomile is mild, apple-flavored, very soothing, and is said to prevent nightmares.

Catnip has a very strong flavor and is said to have been an old-fashioned cough remedy. It is probably best to leave it to your cats.

Dill and fennel are familiar and strongly flavored. Boil the seeds for tea.

Lavender imparts a delicate and unusual fragrance and flavor when mixed with other herbs in tea.

Rose hips are an excellent source of vitamin C and add a fruity, spicy flavor.

Rosemary and sage, both kitchen favorites, are spicy and soothing to sore throats.

Strawberry leaves and fruit make a sweet and fragrant tea.

**Yield:**  7 ounces

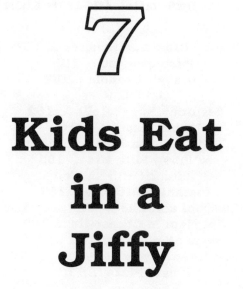

# 7

# Kids Eat in a Jiffy

*If children have easy recipes to prepare, teaching them to make some of their favorite foods in a microwave oven is fun and rewarding. These are some of my favorites and my family's favorites. After you're sure your children can safely manage in the kitchen by themselves, they should be able to concoct these recipes on a Saturday morning while you catch up on extra sleep. You can also make any of these recipes for a quick dinner for the family that's tasty as well as fun.*

## *Recipes and Instructions*

# Fancy Breakfast Squares

*Your kids can make their own breakfast squares by gently microwaving slices of bread and topping each slice with honey, butter, brown sugar, and even cocoa. This is an easy breakfast treat that they'll look forward to on weekends or as a special after-school snack.*

**4 slices white bread**
**4 pats butter or margarine**
**1 tablespoon honey**
**1 teaspoon cinnamon**
**1 tablespoon brown sugar**
**2 tablespoons cocoa**

1   Arrange individual slices of bread on microwave tray and top each one with a pat of butter.

2   Microwave on low for 2 minutes, until butter starts to melt.

3   Spread with honey and sprinkle with brown sugar, cinnamon, or cocoa.

4   Microwave on low for 90 seconds and serve directly from microwave.

**Yield:**   2 servings

# Schmageggies

*Too bad you can't bring your microwave along on camping trips, because that's where Schmageggies taste the best. Your kids may have to pretend that the microwave oven is a friendly campfire, but you can tell them to eat their Schmageggies outside to get the full camping experience.*

**2 hamburger buns**
**2 eggs**
**1 tablespoon butter or margarine**
**1 slice processed cheese**
**Salt and pepper**

1   Scoop out a round piece from the center of the bottom bun, but don't make a hole all the way through the entire bun.

2   Butter inside of hole in the bun. If butter is too hard, you should first soften it by microwaving on low power for 90 seconds and then spread it inside the hole.

3   Carefully break an egg into the hole in each bun and add salt and pepper to taste.

4   Microwave on medium/high power for 4 minutes, check egg for doneness, and continue for 2 more minutes on medium/high power until cooked.

5   When egg is done, top each bun with slice of cheese and microwave on medium for 2 minutes, until cheese melts. Add the top bun and serve.

*Yield:*   2 sandwiches

# Granny's Granola

*You can buy granola in a store, of course, but making it is ten times the fun. Besides being downright healthy, granola recipes let your children experiment with different types of spices and flavors. No two granolas need ever be the same. I like extra cinnamon, my children like extra brown sugar, and my husband likes extra honey.*

*This is also the best kind of recipe to let a child help with in the kitchen, as long as you supervise at the cooking stages. It's fun to mix and mix the dried ingredients, and then mix and mix the oil and honey into them. It's also educational to let a child see what good things can go into a breakfast cereal.*

**4 cups old-fashioned rolled oats**
**1 cup wheat germ**
**1/4 cup instant nonfat dry milk**
**Any combination of the following ingredients to make a**
**total of 4 more cups:**
**Chopped nuts or sesame seeds**
**Sunflower seeds or pumpkin seeds**
**Dried fruit: raisins, apples, bananas, or dates**
**1/2 cup shredded unsweetened coconut**

**1/4 cup vegetable oil or butter**
**1/2 to 1 cup honey**
**1 teaspoon vanilla extract**
**1 teaspoon cinnamon**

1   Combine all the dry ingredients in a large bowl and stir thoroughly to mix.

2   Heat the oil and honey in your microwave on high power for 90 seconds or until they just begin to simmer. Remove from oven and stir in the vanilla.

3   Stir oil-honey mixture into the dry ingredients, making sure to coat all the dry ingredients well.

4   Turn the mixture out into a shallow microwave pan and pat down well. Microwave on high power for 5 minutes, rotate and reduce to medium, and microwave for another 6 minutes. It's a good idea to check the granola every now and then—be careful the top and sides don't cook too quickly. Stir carefully and pat down during the baking.

5   When completely cooled, store in a tightly covered jar or canister. If the weather is very warm or humid, keep in the refrigerator; otherwise, this granola will keep for about a month on the pantry shelf. Do not freeze.

### Variations:

*This recipe can be used as the basis for a crunchy, fruity candy by mixing the cereal with a bit with honey, forming into balls, rolling in sugar, and refrigerating.*

*Granola also makes an excellent topping for your home-made ice cream, pudding, and yogurt.*

**Yield:**   9 or 10 cups

# Granola Rolls

*Once you've made your first few batches of granola, you can combine it into a variety of different types of treats. One of my kids' favorites for morning and lunchtime snacks has always been granola candies—bars or rolls, chocolate chip, peanut butter, raisin-nut-crunch versions—they love them all.*

*Here are recipes for these and other varieties, all using your own lower-cost homemade granola. If you make these rolls up in quantity, you can refrigerate the extra ones, but don't try to freeze them or they will become soggy.*

**2 1/2 cups Granny's Granola**
**1/2 cup confectioners' sugar**
**1/4 cup light corn syrup**

1   Mix ingredients together in a large bowl. When granola is well moistened, shape the mixture into rolls, each about 1 inch in diameter.

2   Transfer rolls to a cookie sheet covered with wax paper or plastic wrap and refrigerate for 1 hour. Slice rolls into individual-size pieces when firm and store, wrapped in plastic, in the refrigerator for up to 2 to 3 weeks.

3   To heat, just pop rolls into microwave and cook for 45 seconds on high power, then let cool. These are perfect on chilly nights with a glass of warm milk.

*Variations:*
*For a different flavor, add 1 cup of chocolate chips, press mixture into a 9-inch-square cake pan, and cut into squares when firm.*

*Or add 1 cup peanut butter to the mixture. Other additions might be 1 cup raisins, 1 cup nuts, or 1 cup peanut butter chips.*

*Try adding 1/2 cup honey and 1 teaspoon vanilla to the granola instead of confectioners' sugar.*

**Yield:**   25 ounces

# Saturday Sweet Rolls

*If your kids like honey and brown sugar and know how to open a package of brown-and-serve rolls, drop pats of butter on top of them, and pop them in a microwave for 2 to 3 minutes, here's a recipe they'll look forward to every weekend. They'll even beg you to stay in bed all morning so they can make their own rolls.*

**1 package brown-and-serve rolls**
**1/2 cup butter or margarine**
**2 tablespoons honey**
**1/4 cup brown sugar**
**1 cup walnut meats or pecans**

1  Place rolls on flat microwave dish and top each roll with pat of butter and spoonful of honey and brown sugar.

2  Microwave on medium/high power for 2 minutes or until butter, honey, and sugar melt.

3  Top with walnuts or pecans.

4  Microwave on medium power for 1 minute. Serve while piping hot.

**Yield:**  8 to 12  rolls

# Maple Biscuits

*Here's a real old-fashioned trail recipe from the Klondike Gold Rush days, updated for modern microwaves. It's so easy, kids can make it themselves in a jiffy.*

**1 cup quick biscuit mix**
**1/2 cup milk or water**
**Maple syrup or other topping**

1   Combine biscuit mix and milk in a bowl and stir with fork until the dough follows the fork around the bowl.

2   Knead the dough a few times just to get the feel of it. With instant mixes, kneading isn't essential, but it's fun for kids anyway.

3   Drop small handfuls of dough onto a flat microwave sheet, making sure to leave enough space between dough drops for them to spread.

4   Microwave on medium power for 4 to 5 minutes, until dough drops feel firm. Your kids will probably overcook the first batch, but tell them not to worry about it. They have to practice with a few batches until they learn how to make consistently sized dough drops.

5   Serve while piping hot. Butter each biscuit right away, microwave on low power for 1 minute to melt the butter, and pour on the syrup. Kids can run through two or three trays before they're satisfied.

**Yield:**   12 biscuits

# Fancy Sparkles

*To make these colored sugars, first refer to the recipe for* **Nature's Colors** *create the colors. Since you are making a food item, choose the familiar edible substances for colors over flowers or herbs, which are best left for coloring craft items. For example, dyes made from beets, cabbage, berries, onion skins, or spinach are preferable to those made from grass, moss, or coffee grounds. Choose the colors you like and don't worry about the flavors mixing with the sugar. Once all the liquid or juice from the flavor has evaporated, the sugar will taste like sugar.*

**3 cups sugar**
**1 cup Nature's Colors (page 90)**

1   Stir sugar and dye together and spread the mixture in a shallow microwave pan. Microwave for 3 minutes on high power; stir, rotate, and microwave on medium for 5 minutes. Remove when the liquid has evaporated. Cool.

2   Store sugar in a tightly covered jar or canister.

*Yield:*   24 ounces

# Rainbow Milk Mix

*Drop a tablespoon or two of this mix into your child's milk and watch the milk turn a pretty shade of pink, yellow, blue, or green. Your child thinks the drink is fun, but you will have added a nice nutritional boost as well. You can also use this mix to make* **Sparkling Saturday Cereal** *as an alternative to the coated cereals that young children like so well.*

**2 cups instant nonfat dry milk**
**1/4 cup Fancy Sparkles (page 164)**
**2 tablespoons protein powder**
**1 teaspoon sugar**
**1/4 teaspon vanilla extract**

Combine the ingredients and store in an airtight canister or a tightly covered jar for up to 4 months. Stir well before using.

### How to Use:

*For fortified milk, add 1 to 2 tablespoons to a glass of cold milk, place in a jar, cover, and shake vigorously. Or place milk and mix in a blender and whirl on high speed 1 minute.*

*For warm milk before bedtime, place a sturdy mugful in the microwave and warm for 2 minutes at high power.*

### Variations:

*For yellow or orange milk, add 1 tablespoon grated orange peel or 1 teaspoon grated lemon peel to the mix.*

*For green milk, add 1 teaspoon dried mint leaves, ground fine between two spoons, to the mix.*

*For pink milk and sophisticated children, add 1 teaspoon dried rose petals, ground fine, to the mix.*

### Idea:

*Add a teaspoon or two to any instant hot cereal mix or your special granola. Add cold milk, heat right in a micro-waveable bowl for 1 minute on high, and swirl to make a marble pattern with a spoon. Return to microwave and heat for an additional minute.*

*Yield:* 19 ounces

# Sparkling Saturday Cereal

*Here's a way to use your **Fancy Sparkles** to brighten up any morning. Make up a batch of this cereal for one of those days when you have a roomful of children and a morning full of cartoons. The cereal is best eaten right away—serve with cold milk and sliced fresh fruit. Extra cereal can be stored in an airtight container for another time or eaten as a snack.*

**2 tablespoons honey**
**1/2 cup Rainbow Milk Mix**
**2 cups plain wheat, corn, or rice cereal**
**1/2 cup chopped dried fruit**
**1/2 cup miniature marshmallow bits**

1   Warm the honey by microwaving on high power for 1 minute in a glass measuring cup.

2   Combine the **Rainbow Milk Mix** with the warmed honey. Pour over the cereal and toss until cereal is completely covered. Stir in the fruit and marshmallows. Serve at once.

*Yield:* 2 to 3 servings

# Instant Hot Cocoa

*Make up quantities of this mix in the nippy days of October and November and you will always have a warm, nourishing drink on hand. For an instant hot pick-me-up, simply add the mix to cold water and boil in microwave. For extra richness, use milk instead of water.*

**2 cups instant nonfat dry milk**
**3/4 cup sugar**
**1/2 cup unsweetened cocoa**
**1 teaspoon salt**
**1 cup miniature marshmallows**

Stir all ingredients together and store in a tightly closed jar or container for up to 2 months.

### How to Use:

*Put 2 to 3 heaping tablespoons of the mix into a mug and fill with water or milk. Microwave on high for 1 minute. Top with whipped cream and cinnamon for a special treat.*

**Yield:** 34 ounces of mix

# Macaroni and Cheese Sauce

*Make **Celestial White Sauce Mix** with butter instead of vegetable shortening and use elbow macaroni for this recipe.*

**1/2 cup Celestial White Sauce Mix (page 150)**
**1/2 cup Cheddar cheese, grated**
**1/2 cup milk**

Combine ingredients, heat in microwave for 45 seconds on high power, and immediately pour over hot elbow macaroni. Toss well.

***Yield:*** 1 1/4 cups sauce

# Hot Ham 'n Cheese-its

*Here's a rainy-day treat that's easy to make and fun to eat. Your kids will like it so much, they'll want to make their own dinners. They can also microwave up a bunch of these for their own lunchboxes and brag that they had to cook their own lunches because Mommy and Daddy were up all night on their computers tracking Eurodollars through the foreign exchange markets.*

**4 slices white bread
8 slices ham
8 slices American cheese
2 teaspoons mayonnaise
Sliced tomatoes**

1   Arrange individual slices of ham on microwave tray and microwave on medium for 1 minute. Set aside ham slices on separate dish.

2   Microwave slices of bread on the microwave tray for 90 seconds on medium/low power.

3   Top each slice of bread with 2 slices of ham, spread with mayonnaise, and top with cheese slices. Microwave on medium for 1 minute or until cheese melts.

4   Top with slices of tomato. Microwave on low power for 90 seconds and serve while still warm. You can store the rest and reheat or eat them cold.

*Yield:*   2 servings

# Freezer Pancake Batter

*This is a perfect mix for microwaveable pancakes because not only does it freeze well, but you can also thaw it in your microwave in a jiffy without losing any flavor. Most store-bought microwave batters are stale or flavorless. This batter, because it is fresh, combines all the ease of off-the-shelf micro-waveable batters with the wholesomeness of fresh-made.*

*Although you can freeze any type of leftover batter, this batter is especially suitable for longer times in the freezer. Freeze this mixture in any kind of container that you can easily pour from, such as a clean milk carton.*

*If you set the batter out to thaw the night before, you will have a very convenient breakfast ready to pour and cook. A frozen container of pancake batter can also be packed in a cooler for overnight camping trips and it will be ready to pour in the morning.*

**2 cups flour**
**1/2 cup sugar**
**4 teaspoons baking powder**
**1/2 teaspoon salt**
**1/2 cup vegetable shortening**
**4 eggs**
**1 3/4 cups milk**

1   Sift dry ingredients into a large bowl.

2   Add the shortening to the dry mixture, cutting it in with a pastry blender or two knives until the mixture is coarsely blended.

3   Add the eggs and milk, stirring until smooth. Next, micro-wave for 30 seconds on low power to blend the flavors and set the batter.

4   Pour into a container for the freezer and cover tightly. Mixture will keep for up to 12 months.

### Variations:
*Add any of the following to the batter before freezing:*

**1 cup fresh or frozen berries**
**2 teaspoons cinnamon**
**2 tablespoons apple, chopped**
**1/2 cup dates, chopped**
*or*
**1/2 cup nuts, finely chopped**

*Stir before using to distribute ingredients evenly.*

### How to Use:
*Melt a tablespoon of butter on your griddle and make the pancakes as usual from the thawed batter. Once the pancakes have cooled, wrap them in microwaveable plastic wrap and freeze. Your children can now reheat them in the microwave whenever they like.*

**Yield:**  12 pancakes

# Soft 'n Savory Bread Slabs

*Kids love bread sticks because they're hot, soft, and as tasty as homemade bread. Thrifty moms like them because they're a good way to use day-old Italian or French bread. You can make these up in bulk, wrap in microwaveable plastic whatever slices you don't eat right away, and freeze the rest. They'll keep for months, and when reheated, the bread tastes fresh again.*

*If you are baking a batch of* **Soft 'n Savory Bread Slabs** *that you have frozen, add 15 minutes to the baking time.*

**1 large loaf Italian or French bread**
**1/2 cup butter, softened**
**2 tablespoons El Paso Seasonings Mix (page 148)**
*or*
**2 tablespoons garlic powder**

1   Slice bread crosswise, making deep parallel cuts, but leaving bottom crust in one piece.

2   Brush all the butter along the cut sides of the bread, top and bottom. Sprinkle on the seasonings of your choice. Put bread back together and wrap tightly in an absorbent paper towel.

3   Microwave on high power for 3 minutes, rotate, reduce power to medium and microwave for 90 seconds. Cut bread into 1-inch-by-4-inch rectangles while it's still warm. Serve immediately.

**Yield:**   4 servings

# Presto Pizza

*Tired of pizza that's cold by the time you drag it home? Too hungry to wait for the pizza man to deliver? Why wait? Why use the microwave just to warm up storebought pizza when you can use the same microwave to make it fresh and fabulous? Here is a handy, thick-crusted pizza so easy to create that even the mature child who has a hankering for pizza can make it unsupervised. Add a little sauce, cheese—and it's a fine after-school snack.*

**2 cups biscuit baking mix**
**1/2 cup cold water**
**1 cup tomato sauce**
**1/2 cup mozzarella cheese, shredded**
**1/2 teaspoon oregano**
**1/2 teaspoon garlic powder**
**Salt and pepper to taste**

1   Mix baking mix and water until a soft dough forms. Roll or pat dough into a 12-inch circle or square on an ungreased microwave cookie sheet. Pinch up edge of circle to form a 1/2-inch rim.

2   Spoon tomato sauce over the dough, then the cheese and seasonings.

3   Microwave on high power for 4 minutes, rotate, and microwave on medium for 3 minutes or until crust is crisp to the touch. If pizza is still not ready, repeat 3-minute cycle on medium power until cheese is bubbling. Be careful not to overcook. If edges are cooking too rapidly, shield them with a circle of paper cut from a brown shopping bag.

## Variations:

Never let not having a certain ingredient stop you from making a pizza. Around our neighborhood, some delicious pizza pies have been made from what many people would consider to be strange items. For example, try brushing the crust with olive oil and topping it with braised broccoli and mushrooms and lots of cheese.

**Yield:** 1 small pizza

# Emergency Pizza

If the urge for pizza strikes and you don't even have baking mix on your shelf, don't despair. You can make a sturdy little pizza from English muffins, bread, even a bagel. If you are using plain white bread for the base, press two slices together and crimp up the crust with your fingers before adding the sauce. If the bread is too stale to manipulate, just sprinkle it with a drop or two of olive oil and microwave it on high for a scant 1/2 minute before adding the fixings.

**Yield:** 1 small pizza

# Snacker Jacks

*If you like popcorn, you'll love caramel popcorn. This treat is an easy one for kids to help you make. If you decide to make this goodie at holiday time or for a child's party, you can wrap individual balls of the corn in brightly colored plastic wrap and tie each with a pretty bow to give away as favors or tree ornaments.*

*It's a good idea to use a microwave-safe popcorn popper when you make up the popcorn in the microwave. If the corn is popped in a bowl or a bag, it might catch fire.*

**1 cup brown sugar, lightly packed**
**1/4 cup butter or margarine**
**1/4 cup light corn syrup**
**1/2 teaspoon salt**
**1/2 teaspoon baking soda**
**15 cups popped corn**

1   Mix the sugar, butter, syrup, and salt in a microwave-safe bowl and cook on high power until blended and until the butter is thoroughly melted and bubbly. Remove from oven and stir in the baking soda.

2   Divide the popcorn onto 2 microwave sheets and pour half the sugar mixture over each, stirring the popcorn as you pour.

3   Microwave on high power for 5 minutes, rotate and stir, and continue on high for another 5 minutes. Cool and store in an airtight container or in individual servings as described above. Mixture will keep well for about 2 weeks.

***Variation:***
*Try adding 1 cup of dry roasted peanuts to the mix before baking, or 1 cup of dried fruit just after you take the corn from the oven.*

***Yield:*** 15 cups

# Homemade "Cracker Jacks"

*Here's another popcorn variation that will be a hit with kids and grown-ups alike.*

**4 cups popped corn**
**1 cup shelled peanuts**
**1/2 cup molasses**
**1/4 cup sugar**

1    Mix popcorn and peanuts together in a large bowl or pan and set aside.

2    Heat molasses and sugar together in the microwave on medium power for 5 minutes and test consistency by letting some of the syrup drop from a spoon into a cup of cold water. The syrup is done when it forms a thread as it drops into the water.

3    Pour hot syrup mixture over the popcorn-nut mixture and stir to coat evenly. Cool and break into chunks with a wooden spoon. Stored in an airtight container, mixture will keep well for up to 4 to 6 weeks.

***Yield:*** 5 cups

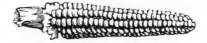

# Midnight Popcorn Munchies

*This one's for those big kids who get to stay up late, but you'll want to share it when you find out how good it tastes. A big bowl of this popcorn is a wonderful accompaniment to an old movie on television. If you want the mixture to be a little sweeter, use plain, dry-roasted peanuts and sweet butter. If you want to add a bit of a salty tang to the mixture, use salted butter and salted peanuts.*

**12 cups popped corn**
**1 1/2 cups peanuts**
**1/2 cup honey**
**1/2 cup butter**

1   Mix popcorn and nuts together in a very big bowl. Set aside. Warm honey and butter together in the microwave on medium power for 3 minutes or until the butter is melted and just starts to bubble. Pour the honey-butter mixture over the popcorn-nut mixture. Toss to mix well.

2   Spread mixture onto a microwave pan and bake on high power for 4 minutes, stir and rotate, then continue on medium for 4 minutes. Cool and break into chunks before serving or storing in an airtight container. Mixture will keep for up to 2 weeks on the pantry shelf.

### Variation:

*A mixture of cashews, walnuts, and other nuts of your choice added to the above recipe will also taste delicious.*

**Yield:**   13 1/2 cups

# Polka-dotties

*Here is a snack recipe you can use as a treat, as a holiday trim for your tree, or as a party favor for children. A candy thermometer is handy for cooking the syrup, but do not put the thermometer into the microwave—test the temperature immediately after removing the bowl.*

**1 cup sugar**
**1/2 cup light corn syrup**
**1/3 cup water**
**1/4 cup butter or margarine**
**1/2 teaspoon salt**
**1 teaspoon vanilla extract**
**16 cups popped corn**
**1 cup gumdrops, jelly beans, or candied cherries**

1    Combine sugar, corn syrup, water, butter, and salt in a ceramic bowl and microwave on medium power for 90 seconds, stir, and repeat until sugar is completely dissolved.

2    Continue to microwave for another 5 minutes on low/ medium or medium power, or  until a candy thermometer inserted in the mixture reads 254 degrees. Mixture is ready when it forms a hard ball when dropped into a cup of cold water. Remove syrup from oven and add vanilla extract.

3    Divide popcorn between two flat pans and pour half of the syrup mixture into each pan. Stir to coat thoroughly.

4    Grease your hands with butter or cooking oil and form popcorn into 4-inch balls while the mixture is still warm. Press gumdrops or other candy onto the surface of the ball. Wrap in clear plastic and tie with a bright ribbon. Balls will keep for up to 2 to 4 weeks.

***Yield:***    10 balls

# Fun Dates

*If your children like dates, they'll love making **Fun Dates.** These stuffed date treats are a little more complicated than some of the other recipes for kids, but they're tastier and give kids a greater sense of accomplishment because they look so hard to make.*

**1 tablespoon butter or margarine**
**1 3/4 cups of confectioners' sugar**
**2 tablespoons frozen orange juice concentrate**
**Pitted dates (about 15)**
**1/2 cup white icing (*see* Mr. Cookie Head, page 181)**

1   Soften butter in glass or ceramic bowl by microwaving on low power for 90 seconds. Add sugar to butter. Stir. Add orange juice concentrate, stir, and microwave on low for 1 minute.

2   Remove from oven and while still warm shape into long, thin strings. Cut the strings into short lengths and press them into the pitted dates.

3   Roll dates in white icing.

4   Microwave on low power for 1 minute and serve while warm or place in refrigerator for 15 minutes and serve chilled. You can also freeze these for summer snacks. If dates get too hard or stale, microwave them on low for 90 seconds to refresh.

*Yield:*   2 servings

# Caramel Ninja Turtles

*When I was a kid, I'd look forward to getting pecan or walnut caramel clusters from the "real" candy store. Then when I discovered I could make them at home in my microwave, my postwar baby-boom heart leapt for joy. Then when I found out the recipe was so simple even a child could make it, I figured better they than I. They make it. I eat it. It's the way of the world.*

**1 cup walnut or pecan pieces**
**1/2 cup caramel squares**
**1/2 cup shredded coconut**
**1/2 cup semisweet chocolate bits**

1   Arrange walnut pieces or pecan pieces in clusters of four pieces each on flat microwave tray. Cover each cluster with a single caramel square.

2   Microwave on medium for 1 minute, or until caramel starts melting and begins to spread.

3   Remove and sprinkle coconut on each cluster.

4   Return to microwave for an additional 30 seconds on medium power. Remove and press 2 chocolate bits (to represent eyes) into turtles.

5   Serve while still warm and chewy. You can store these in the refrigerator and reheat by microwaving on low power for 1 minute.

*Yield:*   12 turtles

# Mr. Cookie Head

*Part of the fun of this recipe is seeing how many different facial expressions your children can design. You may want to designate special shelves in the kitchen that the kids can use for supplies or else you'll find, as others before you have, that creativity knows no bounds and respects no borders.*

**Vanilla wafers, ginger snaps**
**1/2 cup milk**
**2 tablespoons confectioners' sugar**
**1/2 cup of each of the following:**
**Chocolate syrup**
**Shredded coconut**
**Chocolate kisses or pieces**
**Dry roasted or salted peanuts**
**Raisins**
**Mini-marshmallows**

1   Combine milk with 1 tablespoon of the confectioners' sugar to make a thin white icing with the consistency of light cream.

2   Combine the remaining 1 tablespoon confectioners' sugar with chocolate syrup for brown icing. Microwave the syrup on low power for 1 minute to soften if it becomes too brittle.

3   Arrange individual cookies on microwave tray and thoroughly ice each of them with the frosting of your choice.

4   Create faces with raisins or chocolates for eyes, coconut for whiskers or hair, peanuts for other facial features, and mini-marshmallows for hats. Try to make facial expressions as interesting as possible before they are all gobbled up.

**Yield:**   About 24 cookies

# Insta-sweets

*Here's a recipe that allows children to exercise their creativity while satisfying an urge for cookies—any cookies. Just make sure you have all the ingredients on hand because this recipe's so simple, junior bakers won't stop until they've turned everything in the pantry into an insta-cookie.*

**Packaged cookies**
**1/2 cup of each of the following:**
**Crunchy peanut butter**
**Honey**
**Butter**
**Shredded coconut**
**Chocolate kisses**
**Chocolate bars**

1   Arrange packaged cookies on a flat microwave sheet while you combine a scoop of honey, a scoop of peanut butter, and the butter in a bowl (the proportions don't really matter, and they'll vary with each new batch of cookies). Next, soften mixture by microwaving it on low/medium power for 90 seconds to 2 minutes.

2   Spoon the honey-butter mixture onto individual cookies and top cookies with with coconut, chocolate kisses, or pieces of chocolate  bars.

**Yield:** About 20 cookies

# Doughnut Delights

*If your kids have never tasted warm, soft, gooey dough-nuts topped with all sorts of goodies, this recipe will be a real treat and a half. The trick is to use packaged or storebought doughnuts and customize them with whatever is on hand.*

**Packaged or bakery plain doughnuts**
**1/2 cup of any of the following:**
**Peanut butter**
**Marshmallow fluff**
**Maraschino cherries**
**Milk chocolate squares**
**Heath bars**
**Shredded coconut**

Place individual doughnuts on flat microwave tray. Top with one, all, or your favorite combinations of any of these toppings. Microwave on low power until toppings melt.

*Yield:* 2 servings

# S'mores

*Nuthin's better than s'mores. That's all there is to it. Once you've introduced your kids to the taste of a s'more and taught them how to make it themselves in a microwave, you've fulfilled your role as parent. Donna Reed couldn't do any better than this.*

**10 graham crackers**
**1/2 cup crunchy-style peanut butter**
**1/2 cup marshmallow fluff**
**5 chocolate squares or bars**

1   Lay out single graham crackers on a microwave tray.

2   Spread each cracker with peanut butter, top with a chocolate square, a spoonful of marshmallow fluff, and another graham cracker.

3   Microwave on low power for 2 minutes until chocolate melts. Serve while still warm. Store the rest in refrigerator and rewarm in microwave on low power for 3 minutes.

*Yield:* 5 s'mores

# 8

# Holidays in a Hurry

*The microwave oven can make it possible for you to spend more time with your family on holidays by taking the effort out of preparing special holiday items. What used to take hours now takes only minutes with a microwave. I've included a selection of items in this chapter to help celebrate various holidays and seasons throughout the year in a wholesome and simple fashion by using natural ingredients cooked and warmed in your microwave. Some of these items are so simple and fun to prepare that you will want to include your children in on the activities.*

# *Recipes and Instructions*

# Delicate and Fancy Easter Eggshells

*Try these techniques for an Easter egg decorating session that is made possible entirely with materials from your kitchen pantry and hall closets. The colors are natural, the ideas are simple, and whenever you feel especially artistic, you can blow some eggs out of their shells and make permanent decorations. It's especially thrifty to save the shells after a cooking session that called for several fresh eggs.*

*Just remember NEVER to put a raw egg in the shell into the microwave to cook—it will explode and decorate the inside of your oven in a way you'll never forget.*

**6 eggs**
**Lacy patterns: parsley, dill, fern, doilies, or bits of lace**
**Used pantyhose or cheesecloth**
**Rubber bands**
**Outer skins from 4 or 5 yellow onions**
**4 cups water**

1   Blow each egg out of its shell by gently twisting a poultry skewer or sharp awl into the larger end of the egg, through the shell, and into the yolk. Turn the egg upside down over a bowl and carefully chip another, smaller hole in the smaller end of the egg.  Gently blow into the smaller hole until all the egg is in the bowl; wash eggshell and allow to dry.

2   Arrange bits of lacy leaves, lace, or doily designs around each eggshell and wrap the egg and designs in a piece of pantyhose or cheesecloth.  Secure the cloth tightly around the egg with a rubber band.

3   Arrange the eggshells in a glass bowl with the onion skins and cover with water. Bring the water to a gentle boil in the microwave on high power for 3 minutes and simmer eggs and onion skins on medium power for 5 minutes. Remove the pan from the oven and allow the shells to cool in the pan before unwrapping.

### *Variations:*

*Some of the other color treatments described in **Nature's Colors** (page 90) can also be used to boil the eggshells, using cabbage, red onion skins, berries, or beets for a variety of pretty, subtle colors.*

***Yield:***   6 decorated eggs

# Quick Sugar Flowers

*Try making and carefully storing some of these beautiful blossoms and you will never again wonder how to finish off a special cake or dessert. The flowers are sweet, beautiful, and ready to eat. Violets have always been the traditional flower to sugar-coat and eat, but you can also try tiny rosebuds or just the rose petals.*

*It would help to assemble all your supplies and ingredients before beginning this recipe, because you will have to work quickly and with a delicate touch. You will need a small paintbrush and a paper-covered cake rack for drying. Before the advent of microwaves, drying and setting these flowers usually took two or three sunny days. Now, you can make them in 90 seconds flat: just right for the last-minute birthday cake touch.*

**1/2 cup sugar**
**1 egg white**
**Freshly picked blossoms, with stems**

1   Place the sugar in a blender or food processor and process until the sugar is a fine powder. Pour the sugar into a shallow bowl and set aside.

2   Beat the egg white until foamy and pour into a shallow bowl. Paint the egg white carefully on the flower blossom, sprinkle the blossom with the sugar powder, and carefully lay the blossom on the paper to dry. The flowers will dry in the positions you arrange them, so be careful to spread out the petals. Sprinkle with a bit more sugar.

3   Dry the flowers in the microwave on medium power for 90 seconds, and then on low for another 2 minutes if the drying is not complete. Let stand to set.

4   Carefully remove the completely dried flowers and layer them, nestled on tissue paper, in a box. The flowers will keep for up to 6 to 9 months in a cool, dry place.

### *How to Use:*

*Place the flowers on white icing on a wedding or bridal shower cake.*

*Or make **Violets in the Snow**: whip heavy cream with 1 teaspoon vanilla, 1 teaspoon grated orange rind, and 1 teaspoon sugar until stiff. Dot with the violets and serve.*

**Yield:**   8 ounces of blossoms (about 8 flowers)

# Sugars 'n Spice

*For holidays year round, you can enhance the spirit of the season by serving special sugar toppings scented and flavored with herbs and spices. The recipes that follow make holiday desserts special and turn ordinary breakfasts into celebrations. These delicately colored and lightly scented sugars are also an excellent accompaniment to **Herb Teas**, page 153, and are delicious sprinkled on buttered toast or pancakes. Try these sugars to flavor fresh fruit, especially bananas, and to top off applesauce or sliced peaches. For the strongest taste, use freshly grated citrus peel and freshly ground spices, if you have a spice grinder.*

## Citrus and Spice Sugar

**1 cup sugar**
**1 tablespoon orange peel, grated**
**1 teaspoon lemon peel, grated**
**1/4 teaspoon cinnamon**
**1/8 teaspoon nutmeg**
**1/8 teaspoon ginger**

1   Mix all ingredients in a shallow baking pan. Heat in the microwave on medium power for 4 minutes, rotate, and stir. Heat on medium for another 2 minutes. Let stand to cool and allow flavors to blend.

2   Pour mixture into blender and whirl on low speed until ingredients are blended and sugar is ground fine. Stored in a tightly closed container, sugar will keep for up to 6 months.

*Yield:* 9 ounces

# Lemon and Mint Sugar

*This sugar is a tasty addition to ice tea in the summer, or to hot herbal tea in the winter.*

**4 to 5 fresh mint leaves**
**1 cup sugar**
**1 tablespoon grated lemon peel**

1   First dry the mint leaves by chopping them finely, blotting off excess moisture, and microwaving on medium power for 3 minutes. Then mix all ingredients in a shallow microwave pan. Heat on medium power for 3 minutes, rotate and stir, and heat on medium for an additional 2 minutes. Let stand to cool.

2   Pour mixture into blender and whirl on low speed until ingredients are well blended and sugar is finely ground. Stored in a tightly closed container, sugar will keep for up to 6 months.

**Variations:**
*Other herbs you might try drying and combining with sugar are anise, lemon verbena, or rose-geranium leaves.*

**Yield:**  9 ounces

# Vanilla Sugar

*This is one of my favorite recipes. I use it on all types of fruit throughout the year. Sometimes for a not-too-sinful midnight treat, I'll drop two teaspoons of this sugar into a blender with a cup of skimmed milk, whip it up, and enjoy a low-cal vanilla shake.*

*Because the cut-up vanilla beans look rather out-of-place in a jar of pristine white sugar, it's advisable to take special care when serving this sugar or your guests might feel a little squeamish. Pour the sugar into a pretty, shallow bowl and carefully remove the bean pods (put them back into the jar), add a silver demitasse spoon, and put the jar back into the cupbord.*

**2 cups sugar**
**2 vanilla beans**

1   Pour the sugar into a shallow microwaveable mixing bowl. Using kitchen shears or sturdy scissors, cut the vanilla beans into three or four pieces, working directly over the bowl so that all the little black seeds will drop into the sugar. Now microwave on medium for just 1 minute to start the vanilla juices flowing. Immediately pour the cooling sugar into an airtight canister or jar.

2   Cover with a tightly fitting lid and store for 2 to 4 weeks before using. Remove the beans and whirl in the blender for 1 minute if you have lumps in the sugar. Additional plain sugar may be continually added to the container as you use the **Vanilla Sugar** until you notice that the scent  and flavor are gone.

*Yield:*   16 ounces

# Rose Sugar

*This is a sophisticated and pretty sugar that is a pretty addition to a wedding buffet. Add to the romance of the moment by framing the sugar bowl with fresh roses.*

**1 cup sugar**
**1 fragrant rose**

Pour the sugar into a microweavable bowl. Bury the rose in the sugar and microwave on medium power for 1 minute and pour immediately into a clean glass jar with a tight-fitting lid. Place the jar in full sunlight and shake it every other day for 2 to 3 weeks as the flavor works its way through.

**How to Use:**
*You can use this sugar in place of regular sugar in many recipes—the sugar will seem a bit sweeter.*

*This sugar is delightful sprinkled on fresh or brandied fruit or served with one of the **Herb Teas** on page 153.*

*Dust freshly made chocolate or pound cake with the sugar through a fancy doily or try some in **Spiced Coffee**, page 205.*

**Variation:**
*If you would like to try a powdered vanilla or rose sugar, simply place 1 cup of flavored sugar, without the beans or blossoms, into your blender with 1 teaspoon cornstarch and blend on high speed for 2 minutes or until sugar is a fine powder. Let the mixture rest for a week or two before using, to make sure the cornstarch flavor is absorbed.*

**Yield:**   9 ounces

# July 4th Peach Surprise

*Early in the summer, when peaches in the Northeast are still hard to come by, you can get Georgia peaches in the stores. You can rush the happy peach season by poaching the fresh peaches to a soft, fragrant doneness that whets your appetite for the wonderful fresh peaches you will be able to eat right off the tree by the beginning of August. In addition, the yogurt sauce with either the orange marmalade flavor or the melba flavor brightens the sometimes too sweet taste of peaches and honey. Since the yogurt sauce is completely optional, I suggest you serve it on the side.*

**1/2 cup orange juice**
**2 1/2 cups fresh or frozen blueberries**
**1 cup plain yogurt**
**2 tablespoons orange marmalade**
*or*
**2 tablespoons melba sauce**
**1/2 cup water**
**2 1/2 tablespoons honey**
**1 tablespoon lemon juice**
**4 large fresh peaches**

1   Mix orange juice and blueberries in a glass serving bowl, cover, and refrigerate at least 4 hours. You can also make up the mixture the night before and let it sit covered in the refrigerator overnight. Mix the yogurt and marmalade or melba sauce in a small dish, cover, and let it chill through.

2   Combine water, honey, and lemon juice in a glass microwave dish. Peel, pit, and section the peaches into the dish with rest of mixture. Cover and microwave on high power for

4 minutes. Check to make sure peaches are soft. If not, continue on medium/high power for 1 to 2 minutes.

3   Add orange juice and blueberry mixture, stir gently, and chill until ready to serve.

4   Serve with yogurt sauce on the side.

### Ideas:

*This recipe makes a wonderful dessert or late afternoon snack, but you can also serve it topped with wheat germ for a summer breakfast treat, or pack it along for a beach picnic.*

**Yield:**   4 to 6 servings

# Peach Orange Sauce

*Here's a great topping idea for ice cream or crepes. You can use fresh peaches you've put up for the winter or even canned peaches. The neat trick about this sauce is that it's so quick and easy that you can make it as a last-minute idea for a gourmet holiday dinner finale.*

**2 teaspoons cornstarch**
**3 tablespoons confectioners' sugar**
**3/4 cups frozen orange juice concentrate**
**3 1/3 cups fresh or canned peaches**

1   Combine cornstarch and sugar in microwave dish, stir well and add orange juice. Make sure mixture is completely blended.

2   Microwave uncovered on high power for 2 minutes. Stir vigorously. Continue microwaving on high power for 30 seconds or until mixture reaches a rolling boil.

3   Add peaches, stir, cover, and refrigerate for at least 2 hours.

### How to Use:
*Serve over crepes or ice cream. You might also try the sauce over pound or short cake, and top with a thick splash of heavy sweet cream or crème d'Angleterre.*

### Ideas:
*Add 1/4 cup fresh raspberries or microwave frozen raspberries on medium for 30 seconds and pour over top the peach orange sauce and heavy cream.*

**Yield:**   1 1/2 cups

# Holiday Baked Apples

*Baked apples always mean Christmas or Thanksgiving to me. Maybe it's just the snap of the cold weather, the spicy candles, or the hiss of an old-fashioned steam radiator, but the sweet cinnamon-and-apple taste and the soft texture of the fruit remind me of the times my grandmother would spend all day baking apples and letting us sample the juice as they cooked.*

*I don't always have the time to spend in front of a stove, but I want my kids to enjoy some of the foods that were a tradition for me. That's why I developed this microwave version of my grandmother's recipe. I hope you enjoy it as much as I do.*

**2 Granny Smiths or other tart variety of apple**
**2 pats butter or margarine**
**2 teaspons dark brown sugar**
**2 tablespoons fresh lemon juice**
**1/2 cup brandy or Calvados**
**Ground cinnamon**
**Ground cloves (optional)**

1   Core the apples, cut peels away halfway down, and place in microwave dish.

2   Gently place a pat of butter in the center of each apple and cover with teaspoon of brown sugar. Pour lemon juice over each apple and then spoon the brandy into the core and around the sides.

3   Dust each apple generously with the ground cinnamon and a pinch of ground cloves and cover with microwave-safe plastic wrap.

4   Microwave on high power for 3 minutes, rotate 1/4 turn and bake for another 2 to 3 minutes. Apples should be soft but not mushy. Check for doneness and serve.

### *Ideas:*

Add *1/4 cup light cream to apples or top off with a touch of cheddar cheese or Applejack or Calvados.*

*Yield:*   2 servings

# Heavenly Chocolate Fondue

*This is it! Chocolate doesn't get any better than this. Make up this recipe on a gray day and you can dip pieces of pound cake or fresh and frozen fruit to your chocolate-lover heart's content.*

**1 package semisweet chocolate or German chocolate**
**2/3 cup light or dark corn syrup**
**1/2 cup heavy whipping cream**
**Favorite fresh or frozen fruits:**
**Strawberries**
**Dried apricots**
**Raspberries**
**Sliced peaches**
**Dried orange slices**
**Fresh pineapple**
**Cherries**

1   Combine corn syrup and cream in a microwave bowl and microwave on high power for 1 to 2 minutes, or until boiling.

2   Add chocolate, stir through to melt, and microwave again on low/medium power for 90 seconds to smooth and blend.

### How to Use:

*Serve as fondue in a heated carafe and gently dip the fruits on skewers. You can also prepare the chocolate dip in advance of dinner, dip the fruit, roll it in shredded coconut, refrigerate, and serve the coated fruit cold.*

**Yield:**   12 ounces fondue

# Pippins and Port

*This innkeeper's treat has been a tradition for wayfaring travelers on holidays since the time of Queen Elizabeth. The brew is sweet and spicy but has a luxurious creamy headiness from the port. The pippin in this recipe is the apple, and the best apple to use is the Granny Smith. For an especially tantalizing taste, use vintage port for a stronger flavor.*

*This recipe is generous enough for a party-size batch of* **Pippins and Port***, since this dish is traditionally served at the end of a festive dinner to a properly festive crowd.*

**4 cups sugar
4 cups water
2 cinnamon sticks
2 tablespoons ground ginger
2 tablespoons lemon rind
4 pounds apples, peeled and sliced
2 cups port wine**

1   Combine the sugar, water, cinnamon, ginger, and lemon rind in a bowl and microwave on high power for 90 seconds, bringing the mixture to a boil. Simmer on medium power for 3 minutes, remove from the oven, let cool for 2 minutes, strain the syrup, and discard the spices. Cool the syrup thoroughly.

2   Place the apples in a large bowl and cover with the syrup. Cover the bowl with plastic wrap and refrigerate overnight or for at least 8 hours.

3   Simmer the apples and syrup in the microwave on medium power for 5 minutes or until the apples are tender. Remove from oven and cool the apples to room temperature. Stir in the port wine.

### *How to Use:*

*Serve **Pippins and Port** by spooning some of the apples into a serving dish, covering them with the syrup, and topping with sweetened whipped cream.*

***Yield:***   20 servings

# Cranberry Liqueur

*This is one of the finest, prettiest drinks you can serve with your holiday dinner. You can show off the marvelous color best by storing the liqueur in a glass cruet right out on the holiday sideboard, nestled in a bed of evergreens. Highlight the display with spice candles and maybe a touch of wisteria or honeysuckle. The deep ruby color of the cranberry glistens in the candlelight, like a jewel in a setting. The liqueur has a snappy taste that doesn't cloy or linger. You can't taste the vodka, but you can sure feel it.*

**2 cups sugar**
**1 cup water**
**2 cups cranberries, chopped**
**1 teaspoon orange rind, grated**
**1 teaspoon lemon rind, grated**
**3 cups vodka**

1   In a medium-sized ceramic bowl, combine sugar and water and bring to a boil in your microwave on high power for 90 seconds. Reduce to medium and simmer for 3 minutes or until all sugar is dissolved. Remove from oven and stir in cranberries, and orange and lemon rinds. Let cool.

2   Pour cranberry mixture into a sterilized glass jar with a tight-fitting lid. Pour vodka over cranberries and stir. Cover and store in a cool dark place for 4 weeks. Shake container every 4 days or so.

3   Strain cranberry mixture through a cheesecloth or coffee filter and discard pulp. Strain juice two more times or until liquid is clear. Pour into a sterilized quart-size bottle to store. Cover tightly and put back into a cool dark place for another 4 weeks.

**Yield:**   32 ounces

# Instant Raisin Sauce

*Try this sauce brushed on a nice holiday ham before you place it in the oven. Baste the ham with the juices and add additional sauce as the ham bakes. You can add any sort of fruit as a garnish near the end of the cooking time: peaches, pineapple, or raisins and grapes. Because it takes only a minute or so to whip up, you can spice up any leftover chicken as well, even fried chicken if you're so inclined.*

**1/2 cup brown sugar**
**1 tablespoon flour**
**1 tablespoon Hot Peppery Mustard (page 234)**
**1 1/2 cups water**
**1/2 cup cider vinegar**
**1/2 cup raisins**

Mix all ingredients in a microwave bowl, cook on high power for 90 seconds, then medium for 3 or 4 minutes. Store sauce in a sterilized glass jar in the refrigerator. Sauce will keep for up to 2 to 4 months.

### How to Use:

*Brush this sauce as a glaze over ham or poultry. The glaze is best brushed on as you begin to roast, and then refreshed during the roasting process.*

*You can make a delicious gravy by thickening the juices that are flavored with the raisin sauce with 2 tablespoons **Celestial White Sauce Mix**, page 150.*

**Yield:**  2 cups

# Spiced Coffee

*If dinner was special, why not make the coffee that ends the meal special, too? Or, if you're dieting and want to forgo fattening desserts, try one of the following fancy coffees to quell your sweet tooth. This recipe is also an ingenious way to refresh coffee that's been left standing and has cooled or has been in an office thermos for most of the day. I like it because you don't have to brew another batch of morning coffee just to enjoy this end-of-the-day pick-me-up. Were you to buy this as a flavored coffee mix, you could easily spend eight to ten dollars a pound.*

**4 cups brewed or standing black coffee**
**4 whole cloves**
**1 stick cinnamon**

Place the spices in a glass carafe or saucepan, add coffee, and microwave on medium power for 4 minutes. If it starts to boil, reduce power to low, and microwave for another 2 minutes. Let stand at least 90 seconds before serving.

### How to Use:
*Pour the spiced coffee without removing the spices and serve with a dollop of whipped cream dusted with more cinnamon, or try adding a spoonful of **Smooth Orange Cordial** (page 239) or **Coffee Liqueur** (page 238).*

### Variations:
*To freshly brewed coffee, add 1 tablespoon grated orange peel or vanilla extract.*

*Try adding 1 teaspoon **Microwave Chocolate Sauce**, page 229, and topping with crushed mint.*

**Yield:** 4 servings

# Rum Coffee

*Love is like rum; pleasantly intoxicating all night long. Enhance the evening by serving rum coffee to your special guests. This is an alternative to* **Spiced Coffee***, page 205, and is also tasty on those bitter cold nights when the wind is howling about and you want to feel warm all over.*

**3 tablespoons honey**
**1 cup heavy whipping cream**
**3 cups brewed coffee**
**1 pint vanilla ice cream**
**1/2 cup rum**

1   Warm and soften the honey by microwaving it on medium power for 2 minutes. Before it cools, stir the honey into the whipping cream and set the mixture aside.

2   Reheat the coffee in the microwave on high power for 45 seconds, taking care not to let it boil. Pour the hot coffee over the ice cream and stir the honey-cream mixture into the coffee–ice cream mixture. Add the rum and stir well. Serve immediately.

**Yield:**   8 servings

# Instant Mulling Mix

*Here's a holiday variation on mulled cider recipes. It always comes in handy when you want to celebrate the moment for no reason at all. Sprinkle a few tablespoons of this mix over fresh cider before you warm it, or combine it with a quart of hearty burgundy wine for a different-tasting drink. A batch of this mix makes a great winter house-warming gift.*

**1/4 cup orange peel**
**1/4 cup lemon peel**
**2 tablespoons grenadine syrup**
**3 sticks cinnamon**
**2 whole nutmegs, crushed**
***or***
**2 tablespoons ground nutmeg**
**6 whole cloves**
**1/2 teaspoon cardamom**
**3 tablespoons brown sugar**

Finely chop orange and lemon peels. Dry them lightly on medium setting for 2 minutes. Then mix all ingredients together, microwave on low power for 1 minute, rotate, and repeat. Store the mix in an airtight tin or a tightly covered glass jar.

### How to Use:

*Measure 2 tablespoons of mix for every cup of apple cider or wine. Place mix and liquid in a bowl and microwave on high power for 3 minutes to dissolve all solids. Be sure to strain the drink before you pour into individual cups and serve.*

### Idea:

*Try adding a tablespoon or more of one of your homemade fruit brandies for a different flavor.*

**Yield:**   4 ounces

# Spicy Pomander Balls

*These classic hanging balls are pretty to look at and easy to make. They make the holidays very special as they fill your rooms with delightful scents and after the holidays are over, you can hang the balls in your closets to banish stale and musty odors.*

*The microwave adds a new and modern dimension to the tradition of spicy balls: once you've cured the fruit for a week or so, a quick spin in the microwave will thoroughly dry and shrink the balls and they will then last forever. Without this drying step, the balls will sometimes turn moldy after a few weeks.*

*Pomander balls make wonderful gifts when you tie them up with special ribbons or cover them with fancy fabric. You can easily make a nice batch while watching television, and you can use a stack of pomanders that you've piled up to "cure" as a pretty centerpiece for a holiday feast.*

**1 orange, lemon, or apple**
**1/2 cup whole cloves**
**1 tablespoon cinnamon**
**1 tablespoon allspice, ground cloves,**
**nutmeg, or ginger**
**1 teaspoon orrisroot**

1   Working over a bowl, poke small holes into the fruit with a nail or other sharp object. Insert a whole clove into each hole. You can cover the entire surface of the fruit or create a design with the holes; if you plan to hang the pomander ball, remember to leave some space between the cloves to wrap a ribbon around the fruit.

2   Mix the spices and orrisroot in a shallow bowl. Once the fruit is covered with cloves, roll it in the spices until it's completely covered with the mixture. It's a good idea to let the pomander ball sit in the spices for a week or two to cure before microwaving it.

3   During the second week, turn the pomander once or twice a day as it shrinks and the juices mix with the spices in the bowl. When the ball has shrunk, "quick-cure" it to make sure it is thoroughly dried by microwaving it on low for ten minutes and letting it cool and air for a day before hanging in your closet.

### Hints:

*A centerpiece of balls makes a delightful, wonderfully scented arrangement during the holidays.*

*Wrap a ball or two in netting and hang them from your closet rod or give as pretty gifts.*

*If the fragrance of the pomander begins to wane, revive it by warming it in your microwave on low power for for 15 minutes. Then moisten it with few drops of oil of orange and oil of clove.*

**Yield:**   1 ball

# Christmas Wassail

*There are many different recipes for wassail, depending upon which tradition you follow. Scandanavian versions usually contain beer, European varieties may have champagne or another type of sparkling wine, but British and American colonial versions have sherry wine and egg whites. We'll follow the "Charles Dickens" recipe.*

*Originally, the term* wassail *comes from the Old Norse "ves heill" or "Be hale," a traditional Viking toast that had nothing whatsoever to do with Christmas. Through the years, however, this toast became associated with the Christmas season and was extended to describe the holiday punch traditionally served at Christmas gatherings. Therefore, this now festive holiday drink is always served from a fancy punch bowl, and the head of the house should be prepared to give a hale and hearty toast to the season and the new year before serving the drink to his or her guests.*

12 apples, sliced
1 cup water
4 cups sugar
2 tablespoons nutmeg
2 tablespoons ginger
2 tablespoons allspice
6 whole cloves
1/2 teaspoon mace
2 sticks cinnamon
12 eggs, separated
4 cups dry sherry
2 cups brandy

1   Combine the apples, water, and spices in a bowl and microwave on high power for 90 seconds, bringing the mixture to a boil; rotate, reduce to medium power, and microwave for 4 minutes. Cool.

2   Whip the egg yolks and whites separately until the yolks are blended and lemony colored and the whites are stiff. Fold the whites into the yolks.

3   Strain the apple mixture and discard the apples and spices. Blend the juice into the egg mixture.

4   Combine the sherry and brandy in a bowl and bring to a boil in your microwave on high power for 90 seconds. Reduce to medium for 90 more seconds, let cool for 5 minutes, and stir a tablespoon of the warm liquid into the egg mixture. Gradually stir in a few more tablespoons before combining the two mixtures completely.

### *Idea:*

*Surround the wassail bowl with holly and candles and float some baked apples stuffed with brown sugar directly in the brew.*

**Yield:**  11 cups

# Christmas Currant Punch

*The exotic taste of crème de cassis liqueur is the punch in this punch. Cranberry juice cocktail adds to the spiciness, but it's the black currants that will make your guests want the recipe for next year's round of Christmas houseparties.*

**3 cups water**
**3 cinnamon sticks**
**8 slices fresh gingerroot, unpeeled**
**10 whole cloves**
**6 cups cranberry juice cocktail**
**1 1/2 cups orange juice**
**3 tablespoons fresh lemon juice**
**2 cups crème de cassis**
**1/2 cup apple schnapps**
**4 thinly sliced orange quarters**
**Cinnamon sticks for drink stirrers**

1   Combine water, cinnamon sticks, gingerroot, and cloves in microwave bowl and microwave on high power for 3 minutes. Reduce to medium power for 6 minutes or until only 1 or 2 cups of the original liquid remain.

2   Add cranberry juice, orange juice, lemon juice, schnapps, and crème de cassis and microwave on low power for 2 minutes to heat through. Remove from heat but don't cool completely. Serve with orange slices and cinnamon sticks.

*Yield:*   12 cups

# Christmas Glögg

*When the Swedes celebrate Christmas, they mull their red wine with spices and tangy berries to brighten up the Arctic winter. Now you can bring this tradition to America with a quick microwave version of this holiday treat.*

**1 quart cranberry juice cocktail**
**4 cups granulated sugar**
**1/2 lemon**
**9 whole allspice berries**
**6 whole cloves**
**3 whole cinnamon sticks**
**1/4 teaspoon ground cinnamon**
**1/4 teaspoon ground ginger**
**Pinch of nutmeg**
**1 lemon, sliced**
**1 orange, sliced**
**1/2 cup raisins**
**4 quarts dry American burgandy or claret**
**Cinnamon sticks for drink stirrers**

1   Combine the first 9 ingredients in a large bowl. Plan to microwave the liquid in 2-cup batches.

2   Microwave each batch of the mixture on high power for 4 minutes to bring to a boil and then on medium power for 5 minutes to simmer gently. Remove and let cool. Strain through cheesecloth or fine strainer to remove any solids.

3   Just before serving, add wine, lemon and orange slices, and raisins. Microwave on low power for 3 minutes to warm, and garnish with cinnamon stick stirrers.

***Yield:***   20 cups

# New Year's New Potato Salad

*Here's a great recipe for New Year's Day, the day after Thanksgiving, or any "day after" when you want a super dish to make your holiday leftovers look and taste better.*

**1 1/2 pounds thin-skinned red potatoes**
**1/4 cup water**
**4 slices of bacon**
**1/2 onion, finely chopped**
**1/2 cup celery, chopped**
**2 teaspoons flour**
**1 teaspoon sugar**
**3/4 teaspoon salt**
**1/4 teaspoon pepper**
**1/2 cup chicken broth**
**2 tablespoons red wine vinegar**

1   Arrange potatoes in a circle around the edge of a flat microwave dish. Puncture and sprinkle lightly with water to keep them from drying out in the cooking and cover with microwave-safe wrap. Microwave on high power for 9 minutes, turning potatoes every 3 minutes. Remove and let stand for 10 minutes. Drain after 10 minutes.

2   While potatoes are draining, rack the bacon over a microwave dish that will catch the drippings during cooking. You can also microwave the bacon directly in its own drippings. Microwave on high power for 4 minutes, remove, and drain on paper towel.

3   Add onion and celery to drippings. Cover and microwave on high power for 3 minutes to make them crisp yet tender.

Stir in salt, flour, sugar, and pepper. Cover and microwave for 1 minute on high power. Stir in chicken broth and vinegar and microwave uncovered on high for 5 minutes to thicken the mixture.

4   Slice potatoes and add them along with most of the bacon to the mixture. Stir to coat with broth and seasonings. Cover and microwave on high for 1 minute and garnish with the rest of the crumbled bacon.

### *How to Use:*

*Potato salads are the perfect dishes for any meals that involve leftovers. This potato salad is also perfect for the New Year's Day football crowd around the television set.*

*Yield:*   4 cups

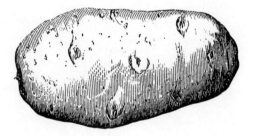

# 9

# Gifts in a Twinkling

*If it's the thought that counts, then giving gifts you've made yourself shows your thoughtfulness as well as your skill. Maybe you like to plan your handmade gifts many months in advance. Or, like many people, you may think of an idea or a quick gift as a spur-of-the-moment act of thoughtfulness. Either way, here are some ideas that will guarantee success. All of these projects are quick enough to make in your microwave to take advantage of a special occasion or opportunity to be thoughtful—and most of them will save you money in the process.*

# Recipes and Instructions

# Rose Beads

*One of the oldest forms of personal fragrance, rose beads are also a modern, natural way to please yourself and people around you. These beads are meant to be worn against the skin so that the warmth of the body will release their fragrance gently and magically. It's one of the most wonderful, romantic ideas I've seen in a long time—make a batch of these for yourself, or as a very special bon voyage gift for a woman traveling to a warm, sunny climate, where they will feel wonderful against tanned skin.*

**4 cups rose petals**
**Essential oil or perfume (optional)**
**Toothpicks**
**Nylon fishing filament or baby ribbon**

1   Place the rose petals in an enamel or a glass bowl and cover with warm water. Set microwave to medium power for 2 minutes and then to low for an additional 15 minutes. Do not allow the liquid to boil. Cover and cool overnight.

2   Repeat the cooking process three more times. Add a drop of oil or perfume, if desired, just before cooking for the last time. You should have a smooth, soft paste by now; if not, continue cooking until all the liquid is absorbed. Let paste cool completely.

3   Moisten your fingers with a few drops of essential oil or perfume and pinch off a bit of the paste. Roll it into a ball, pierce the ball all the way through with a toothpick, and place the bead and toothpick on a piece of plastic wrap to dry. Continue until all the paste is used and allow the beads to dry on the toothpicks for 3 hours.

4   Carefully remove the toothpicks and allow the beads to dry overnight. Thread a needle with the nylon fishing filament or baby ribbon and string the beads into a necklace long enough to fit over the head.  Knot the ends securely and cut off any excess ribbon or filament.

### Ideas:

*If you don't have enough rose petals, try mixing other fragrant flower petals in with the roses. Try tinting the mixture with a few drops of **Nature's Colors**, page 90, if you want vividly colored beads, but remember that the color may rub off along with the fragrance.*

### Tip:

*While you are collecting enough rose petals to boil, keep them in an open container like a basket or an open tin in a sunny location. Toss the petals once or twice a day as you gather enough for your recipes. A closed container or a dark storage place will encourage mold to form and the fragrance will be lost.*

**Yield:**   One 12-inch necklace

# Meaty Treats for Dogs and Cats

*Your pet can share in the microwave gift-giving fun at every holiday season with this simple recipe. This is a treat for all those times when your pet deserves a special favor. No need to run to the pet store or the supermarket when you can make it yourself. This is also a way to use up those parts of poultry that usually get tossed aside. If the members of your family aren't especially fond of eating things made from that bag of organs found in chickens or turkeys, you can be sure that your pet dog or cat will love the biscuits made from those parts.*

*When making this recipe for a cat, shape the biscuits into tiny bits for easy chewing, and don't be too disheartened if your cat acts finicky—my cat won't touch "dog" food.*

**1 pound liver, organs, or other meat
(enough to make 2 cups cooked meat)
2 cups bran
2 cups old-fashioned oatmeal
1/4 cup cooking oil**

1   Cover meat with cold water and place in the microwave. Bring to a boil on high power for 3 to 4 minutes. Reduce to low for 6 minutes. Remove meat from water and let cool; retain water.

2   When meat is completely cool, chop into 1-inch pieces and grind in food processor, chop in blender, or process through a meat grinder until it is finely ground.

3   Mix ground meat, bran, oatmeal, and oil, adding the cooking water from the meat as necessary to make a thick

dough. Try to avoid adding any more liquid than you need to make a dough that is coarse and just wet enough to work with.

4   Shape the dough into flattened balls or little bone shapes and arrange in a flat microwave dish.

5   Microwave on low/medium or low power for 10 to 15 minutes, depending upon your microwave setting. When timer goes off, check for doneness and let stand for another hour to make sure biscuits are sufficiently hard and crunchy.

6   Let the biscuits air dry for 24 hours and store in a labeled, closely covered container in the pantry for up to 4 weeks.

*Yield:*   3 pounds

# Microwave Oven Freshener

*Mix up a batch of this potpourri and place it in the micro-wave oven to simmer whenever you want to freshen your oven without scrubbing. You will also have a nice burst of fragrance the second you open the oven door. It's a most homey mixture to use and to give, and it's especially pleasing in the dead of winter.*

**1/4 cup pine needles**
**1 tablespoon whole cloves**
**1/2 cup lemon, orange, or tangerine peel**
**2 cinnamon sticks**
**1 tablespoon allspice**

Combine all ingredients and store in a glass jar or pretty tin, tightly covered.

### *How to Use:*
*Add a tablespoon of the mix to 2 cups water and let mixture simmer gently in your microwave on low to medium power for 1 to 2 minutes.*

### *Tip:*
*Because this mixture is not edible, be sure to label it and store it away from food.*

*Keep some on your regular stove or wood stove in a sturdy pan of water for a pleasing fragrance all through the kitchen, as well.*

**Yield:**  8 ounces

# Instant Freezer-fresh Fruit Preserves

*When you microwave and freeze your fruit jams and preserves, you save yourself all the trouble of hot-water canning, adding paraffin, and making sure the seals are secure. If you have a lot of freezer space, you can enjoy a very fresh-tasting preserve.*

*You will have to plan ahead if you want to make preserves as Christmas gifts, but you will find it is well worth it. All through the winter and the holidays, nothing is more welcome than fruit that tastes as fresh as summer.*

**4 cups strawberries**
**8 cups sugar**
**1 1/2 cups water**
**2 tablespoons fruit pectin**
**2 tablespoons lemon juice**

1   Clean berries, place in a large bowl, and crush them a bit. Add sugar and stir gently to mix. Let berries stand for 10 minutes.

2   Combine water and pectin in a glass microwave bowl and bring to a boil on high power for at least 90 seconds. Stir, reduce power to medium for 90 seconds. Remove and stir again.

3   Pour water-pectin mixture over the strawberries and stir to mix and to mash the berries a bit more. Stir in the lemon juice.

4   Pour the fruit into freezer containers or sterilized glass jars, leaving room for expansion. Cover and let sit at room temperature overnight.

5   Refrigerate one jar for immediate use if desired and freeze the other containers. Preserves will keep for up to 9 months in the freezer.

### *Variations:*

*Many other fruits can be made into quick freezer preserves. For example, try freezing freshly crushed blueberries, raspberries, or cranberries and chopped lemon.*

*Yield:*   10 cups

# Apple Butter

*Apple butter is a warm, earthy, and natural spread that turns any bread or cracker into a special treat. You can prepare a light apple butter or a richer spread, depending upon the amounts of spices you use. This is a tart, very spicy apple butter, so the seasonings in this recipe may seem too heavy for those used to a milder butter.*

*You might want to try the recipe with half the cinnamon, cloves, and allspice and taste to see if you want to add more. Because your microwave is so fast, I suggest you make up the whole batch according to the following recipe, preparing it in smaller portions to fit into the microwave. Then refrigerate or freeze in small portions so you can use it throughout the year.*

**8 pounds ripe apples**
**2 cups apple cider**
**3 cups brown sugar, firmly packed**
**3 tablespoons cinnamon**
**1 teaspoon allspice**
**1 teaspoon ground cloves**

1   Peel, core, and slice the apples. Place apples in a large bowl, pour the apple cider over them, and microwave separate smaller portions on medium power for 2 minutes and then on low until they are tender, about 10 minutes in all. Check frequently, however, to make sure the apples don't stick and burn.

2   When apples are soft, remove them from the oven and let cool. To strain and mash them, you can either press them through a sieve or place the apples and juice in a food processor and whirl them until you have a smooth mixture.

3   Return the pureed apples and juice to a glass bowl or saucepan and add the spices. Microwave on medium power for 5 minutes, stir, and microwave for 5 minutes more or until mixture begins to bubble and thicken. Remove from oven and cool.

4   Pour apple butter into sterilized glass jars, cover, and store in the refrigerator. Or, leave some room for expansion in the jars and freeze. Apple butter will keep for 2 to 4 weeks in the refrigerator and up to 9 months in the freezer.

### *Variations:*

*Try the same recipe, but substitute pears or peaches for the apples, and instead of apple cider, use a mixture of 2 cups water and 1/2 cup lemon juice. Use half the spices, or spice to your taste.*

**Yield:**   13 cups

# Tam o' Shanter's Butterscotch

*Even the mighty Douglass would put up his broadsword for a taste of this traditional Scots sauce floating on a dish of heavy double cream. This sauce is simple, relatively quick, and will keep for up to 3 months in the refrigerator. Serve it over ice cream, of course, or warmed over in milk.*

**2 cups brown sugar, packed
2 tablespoons flour
1/2 cup butter, melted
1 cup boiling water
2 teaspoons vanilla extract**

1   Melt the butter in your microwave on high power for about 90 seconds, until it starts to bubble. Remove immediatelyif it starts to burn.

2   Keep the butter warm on the lowest oven setting while mixing the sugar and flour together in a bowl. Remove butter from oven and slowly add it to the flour and sugar mixture.

3   Microwave mixture for 5 minutes on low power until the butter takes on a golden yellow hue. Remove from oven.

4   Slowly add the boiling water to the mixture, stirring constantly. Cook mixture for 2 minutes on low power.

5   Remove from oven; stir in vanilla. Pour while still warm into sterilized glass jars. Allow to cool before refrigerating; sauce will keep for 3 to 6 months in the refrigerator.

*Yield:*   2 cups

# Microwave Chocolate Sauce

*For the chocolate lover in your family, here's a recipe that will satisfy a midnight craving in a jiffy. This basic sauce can be varied in hundreds of ways, depending on your audience and on the fancy ingredients you have on hand. Once you have developed your own chocolate specialties (see **Variations** for some ideas to start you off), package your special sauce in small, pretty jars and add them to some of the **Gift Baskets** described in Chapter 10.*

**2 ounces semisweet baking chocolate**
**2 tablespoons butter**
**1/4 cup water**
**1 1/2 cups sugar**
**Dash salt**
**1 teaspoon vanilla extract**

1   Microwave chocolate on medium power for 2 to 4 minutes to melt.

2   Stir in butter, water, sugar, and salt. Microwave on medium power for 2 minutes, then low power for 3 minutes. Stir in vanilla.

### How to Use:

*This sauce is best when served warm. Either serve immediately after making or reheat in a microwave oven for 1 minute on high.*

*To store, pour into sterilized glass jars. Allow sauce to cool before refrigerating. This sauce will keep for 6 months in the refrigerator.*

*Variations:*
*Add any of the following flavorings in place of or in addition to the vanilla in Step 2:*

**1 teaspoon orange extract**
*or*
**1/3 cup orange juice**
**1 teaspoon mint extract**
**1/4 cup strawberries or raspberries, crushed**
*or*
**1/4 cup raisins or nuts, chopped**
**1 tablespoon Holiday Crème de Menthe (page 235),**
**Coffee Liqueur (page 238),**
**Smooth Orange Cordial (page 239),**
*or*
**Grand Marnier**
**1 teaspoon instant coffee**

# Hot Fudge Sauce

**1 cup sweetened condensed milk**
**1 cup sugar**
**1/4 cup light corn syrup**
**4 tablespoons butter**
**5 ounces semisweet baking chocolate**
**1 teaspoon vanilla extract**

1   Melt chocolate on medium setting for 3 to 4 minutes. Combine all ingredients and heat on low for 4 minutes; stir until the mixture is completely smooth, reheating if necessary on low for 2 minutes to make sure all the chocolate is melted.

2   Cool and store it in a sterilized glass jar in the refrigerator for up to 4 weeks. Let it warm to room temperature before using.

*Yield:*  2 cups

# Sweet Berry Syrups

*Berry syrups are great all-around instant snacks as well as personalized gifts. If you have a garden, you can preserve the fresh taste of spring year round. If you live near a farmer's market, you can celebrate harvest at Christmas time or for friends' birthdays.*

*The syrups are versatile as well as tasty. You can use them on pancakes make from **Freezer Pancake Batter**, page 170, or on crepes, or as the basis for natural sodas. In addition, they taste wonderful over vanilla ice cream or swirled through vanilla pudding.*

## Blueberry Syrup

**3 cups blueberries**
**3 cups sugar**
**1 cup water**
**1/4 cup lemon juice**

1   Wash and drain blueberries. Crush the berries in a bowl, or process for 1 minute in a food processor or blender to make a berry puree. Add sugar.

2   Microwave puree on medium power for 4 minutes, stir, microwave for 3 minutes.

3   Remove from oven and stir in the lemon juice before puree cools.

4   Strain the mixture through a coffee filter or cheesecloth and pour the syrup into a sterilized jar. Discard the pulp or use it in your garden compost. Cool the syrup before using and store in the refrigerator for up to 6 months.

## Variations:

Almost any kind of berry can be substituted for the blueberries. You can add half the sugar called for, taste, and add more sugar if you think the berries will need more sweetening.

## Idea:

A natural soda is a healthy way to wean your children from the more expensive, store-bought kind. Simply add one tablespoon of syrup to an 8-ounce glass of seltzer, club soda, or mineral water for a refreshing drink.

**Yield:**  4 cups

# Mr. Mustards

*Not everybody likes mustard, but those who do will go to any lengths to try new and different mustard varieties. This recipe is especially tangy and it can be varied according to taste. The ingredient that gives the tang is different in the two recipes which follow. You might like the zip of horseradish over the bite of cayenne—try the versions given here and invent your own from these ideas.*

*These mustards make fantastic gifts, either alone or in combination with other spices and cheeses. Plan ahead for gift giving by saving pretty containers and crocks for the mustards, but do not freeze these mixtures.*

## Spicy Horseradish Mustard

**1 cup dry mustard**
**3/4 cup white wine vinegar**
**1/3 cup water**
**1/4 cup sugar**
**3 tablespoons brown sugar, lightly packed**
**2 teaspoons onion salt**
**1 teaspoon caraway seeds**
**2 eggs**
**1 tablespoon horseradish**

1   Combine all ingredients except eggs and horseradish in a glass or ceramic bowl and microwave on low power for 15 minutes so that the flavors will blend. Cover and let stand at room temperature overnight.

2   In a separate bowl, lightly beat the eggs; then stir them into the mustard mixture. Microwave the mixture on low power for 3 minutes, stir, and microwave on low for 2 minutes more or until the mixture thickens.

3   Stir in the horseradish and cool for 10 minutes. Pour into a sterilized jar and refrigerate for 24 hours before using. Mustard will keep in the refrigerator for up to 3 months.

*Yield:*   16 ounces

# Hot Peppery Mustard

2/3 **cup beer**
1/2 **cup dry mustard**
2 **tablespoons water**
1 **tablespoon sugar**
2 **teaspoons white wine vinegar**
1 **teaspoon salt**
1 **teaspoon cayenne pepper**
1/2 **teaspoon turmeric**
1/2 **teaspoon ginger**
1 **egg**

1   Combine all ingredients except egg in a glass bowl and microwave on low power for 4 minutes. Cover and let stand overnight at room temperature.

2   In a separate bowl, lightly beat the egg, then stir it into the mustard mixture. Microwave the mixture on low power for 3 minutes, stir, and microwave for 3 more minutes or until the mixture thickens.

3   Remove from oven and cool for 10 minutes. Pour into a sterilized jar and refrigerate for 24 hours before using. Mustard will keep in the refrigerator for up to 3 months.

### Variation:
*Replacing the sugar with the same amount of honey will give a smooth, different flavor.*

*Yield:*   16 ounces

# Holiday Crème de Menthe

*This recipe requires extra time for the ingredients to cure, so plan ahead. Crème de menthe is another holiday treat that people look forward to year after year. This favorite after-dinner drink is a good addition to chocolate sauces and desserts. It's refreshing in the summer poured over ice and topped with a few sprigs of fresh mint.*

**4 tablespoons fresh mint leaves**
**1 fifth vodka**
**4 cups sugar**
**2 cups water**
**10 drops peppermint oil**
**2 to 3 drops green food coloring (optional)**

1   Crush mint leaves in a mortar and pestle or place them between a tablespoon and a teaspoon and macerate. Place crushed leaves in a sterilized glass jar and pour vodka over them. Cover and let sit for 10 days.

2   Strain vodka through cheesecloth or a coffee filter and discard mint.

3   Make a syrup of the sugar and water by dissolving the sugar in the water in the microwave on high power for 4 minutes. Let mixture cool. Add syrup to the mint-flavored vodka; add peppermint oil and food coloring, and stir.

4   If liqueur is not clear, you may want to filter it a second time. You may also want to omit the green food coloring. Liqueur will keep for a year on the pantry shelf.

**Yield:**   48 ounces

# Homemade Scotch Liqueur

*Bonnie Prince Charlie might have liked to take a nip of something similar to this before he went off to battle, but what took his vintners years to age will only take you a week or two. This mixture is smooth and as inexpensive as whatever type of Scotch you choose to use. The anise extract is something of a specialty item, but you should be able to find it in a gourmet store or a large, well-stocked grocery store.*

**2 cups sugar**
**1 cup water**
**1 teaspoon anise extract**
**1 pint Scotch**

1   Dissolve sugar in water to make a syrup by microwaving on high power for 4 minutes. Watch mixture closely so that it doesn't bubble over. Reduce to medium power for 3 minutes or until the mixture becomes syrupy. Remove and let cool.

2   Pour sugar syrup into a sterilized quart-size bottle. Add anise and Scotch. Stir gently and cover.

3   Let mixture age in a cool, dark place for 1 to 2 weeks before serving.

***Yield:***   32 ounces

# Homemade Galliano

*Galliano is a fun liqueur that's been the subject of many jokes. You can float Galliano on a screwdriver to make a Wall-banger, or you can sip it as an after-dinner treat with coffee. This liqueur is known by its bright yellow color, but it can also be made without adding the food coloring, if you prefer.*

**2 cups sugar
1 cup water
1/4 cup anise extract
1 teaspoon vanilla extract
3 drops yellow food coloring
1 fifth vodka**

1   Dissolve sugar in water to make a syrup by microwaving on high power for 4 minutes. Reduce to medium power for 3 minutes or until the mixture becomes syrupy. Remove and let cool.

2   Pour sugar-water syrup into a sterilized quart-size bottle. Add anise extract, vanilla, and food coloring. Stir gently and add the vodka.

3   Cover and let the mixture sit for 10 days to 2 weeks before serving.

*Yield:*  42 ounces

# Coffee Liqueur

*Here's another special treat to serve your guests or family during the holiday season or any time you just want to relax and enjoy the moment. You don't even have to brew the coffee especially for the recipe. Any leftover coffee will do because you will refresh it in the microwave with the flavorings. This drink is welcome with coffee and dinner mints.*

**4 cups sugar**
**6 cups very strong coffee**
**1/2 vanilla bean**
**1 fifth vodka**
**1 tablespoon Microwave Chocolate Sauce (page 229)**

1   Dissolve sugar into the coffee by cooking on high power for 3 minutes in the microwave, bringing mixture to a vigorous boil. Let cool.

2   Chop vanilla bean into small pieces, being very careful to keep the little seeds. Place the pieces in the bottom of a large sterilized glass jar and pour in the vodka.

3   Add cooled sugar-coffee mixture and chocolate sauce. Stir and cover container; let mixture rest for 30 days. Strain twice through cheesecloth or a coffee filter. Liqueur will keep well for several months on the pantry shelf.

**Yield:**   10 cups

# Smooth Orange Cordial

*Try a teaspoon of this delicious liquid mixed into your* **Microwave Chocolate Sauce**, *page 229, before you spoon it over ice cream, or swirl a spoonful into hot coffee and top with whipped cream, or add some to a cup of hot tea and make it into a special, heartwarming treat.*

**6 oranges
2 cups vodka
1 cup brandy
1 teaspoon cinnamon
1/2 teaspoon allspice
1/2 teaspoon nutmeg
2 whole cloves
2 cups sugar
2 cups water**

1   Wash and rinse oranges well and carefully peel them, avoiding the bitter white pith under the peel. Chop the peel and place it in a sterilized quart-size glass jar.

2   Add the vodka, brandy, and spices, cover the jar, and place in a cool, dark place for 2 weeks. Shake the bottle twice a week to mix contents.

3   Strain the mixture through a cheesecloth or coffee filter and discard the orange peel or use it to make **Chewie Citrus Candies**, page 247.

4   Dissolve the sugar in water by bringing to a boil in the microwave on high power for 3 minutes. Cool.

5   Stir the sugar-water mixture into the strained orange-liqueur mixture, pour the liquid into a sterilized glass bottle and cap securely. Store in a cool, dark place for 2 to 4 weeks.

**Yield:**   40 ounces

# St. Valentine's Pear Cordial

*Pears were often served at wedding feasts for their aphrodisiacal qualities and that's how they came to be called St. Valentine's fruit. This very sweet, somewhat unusual cordial is also a delicious accompaniment to fresh apples in the fall. If you start this cordial just when the first pears of the summer are in, you will have a delightful treat in just a few months.*

**1/2 cup water**
**1 cup sugar**
**4 ripe, firm pears**
**4 whole cloves**
**1 teaspoon allspice**
**1 teaspoon nutmeg**
**4 cups vodka**

1   Dissolve sugar in water by microwaving on high power for 3 minutes; remove and cool. To reduce the alcohol content of the vodka, you can add it to the sugar-water mixture and microwave on medium power for two minutes. To keep the vodka at full strength, add it directly to the pears.

2   Do not peel the pears, but slice them into large pieces and place them in a sterilized 2-quart-size glass jar. Sprinkle on the cloves and spices and stir in the sugar-water and vodka. Cover and store in a dark place for 10 weeks. Turn the jar upside down to mix the contents once a week.

3   Strain mixture through a cheesecloth or coffee filter and discard the pulp. Pour the liquid into a sterilized glass bottle, cap securely, and store for 2 weeks in a cool, dark place.

*Yield:*   36 ounces

# Purple Cordials

*Plums, like pears, were treated as aphrodisiacs by the ancient physicians. One sip of this cordial and you'll see why. This brew has a very long storage time, so plan on serving or giving it as a gift one whole season after making it. The longer it is stored, the richer the flavor, so don't rush this one. After six months, it's at its best for drinking, and it will keep well for another 6 months after that.*

**3 pounds ripe plums**
**2 cups sugar**
**1 quart vodka**

1   Pit plums and slice them. Place plums into a microwave bowl along with sugar and vodka. Microwave on low power for 2 minutes. Stir thoroughly and microwave for 2 minutes on medium power to bruise the plums and start the flavors cooking. Then transfer entire mixture to a sterilized glass quart-size jar, stir to further bruise the plums, add vodka, and cover. Let mixture sit for 2 weeks.

2   Strain through a cheesecloth or coffee filter and discard plums. Pour juice into a sterilized container, cover tightly, and store for 2 to 4 more months, or until mixture is clear.

*Yield:* 32 ounces

# Prune Cordial

*Ancient medics prescribed prune cordials after dinner to aid the digestion. Prune cordials were snappy and flavorful and often taken right before bedtime. Of all the cordial recipes, this one is possibly the easiest to make, and certainly the ingredients are available all year long. It's a great gift for someone who has always thought the lowly prune was only good for snacking.*

**1/2 pound dried prunes**
**Water to cover prunes**
**1 pint whiskey**
**2 teaspoons sugar**

1   Microwave prunes in water for 2 minutes on medium power and then 3 minutes on low power. Drain and discard water.

2   Place prunes in a sterilized quart-size glass jar with whiskey and sugar. Stir to mix. Cover and let mixture sit for 2 weeks.

3   Strain mixture through cheesecloth or a coffee filter and discard fruit. Store the juice in a sterilized glass jar, corked or capped tightly, for up to 1 year on the pantry shelf.

*Yield:*  16 ounces

# Sweet Berry Cordial

*This cordial is a wonderful way to preserve the taste of early summer, when the berries are at their first blush. Pie cherries are tart and remind me of Father's Day, when the whole world is green and soft. Raspberries remind me of the Fourth of July. And black cherries remind me of a lazy August afternoon. If fresh berries give you the same feelings of joy, then this cordial is just what you—or your lucky recipient— will need on a dreary, dark November day.*

*This brew is a cheery color and looks fantastic in a cut-glass cruet. Look in antique shops for pretty containers for all your cordials and liqueurs, and at holiday time you can arrange them like liquid jewels on the sideboard or nestled in evergreen branches on top of the liquor cabinet.*

**2 cups sweet black cherries**
**1 cup pie cherries**

**1 cup raspberries**
**3 cups vodka**
**4 cups sugar**
**1/4 cup lemon juice**
**2 cups water**

1   Gently mash cherries and raspberries together. If you don't have pie cherries, use 3 cups of sweet cherries instead, and reduce the sugar by 1/2 cup. Don't worry about removing the pits or seeds. Put fruit mash into a bowl and microwave on low power for 3 minutes. Scrape mash into a clean, half-gallon-size jar.

2   Pour vodka over the fruit, cover, and let the mixture sit in a dark place for at least 4 weeks. Shake fruit every other day or so without opening the jar.

3   Microwave sugar, lemon juice, and water together on high power for 1 minute or until sugar is dissolved; let cool.

4   Strain fruit-vodka mixture through cheesecloth or a coffee filter. Press out all the juice and discard the pulp. You should have at least 4 cups of juice.

5   Stir in the sugar-water syrup and pour into clean glass bottles. Cap or cork with new corks and let the brew sit for another 2 weeks before serving. Liqueur will keep indefinitely in a cool, dark place.

*Yield:*  48 ounces

# Blueberry Cordial

*Blueberries are like a celebration of life. They are fresh, bright, and full of summer skies, even in the gray of winter. They are like a remembered day in the country. If you're lucky enough to have more blueberries than you know what to do with, this cordial is a good place to start. This is one of the prettiest-looking cordials that you can make, so celebrate its lovely hue by finding a wonderful decanter or cruet to show it off with. The secret to a clear cordial is in the straining, so be sure to follow the directions exactly.*

**4 cups blueberries**
**3 cups vodka or gin**
**1/4 cup lemon juice**
**1 1/2 cups water**
**4 whole cloves**
**1/2 teaspoon coriander seeds**
**3 cups sugar**

1   Wash and drain the blueberries. Crush them in a bowl, blender, or food processor and add lemon juice, water, cloves, and coriander. Microwave the mixture on medium power for 1 minute and low power for 2 minutes. Even before it cools, scrape the mash into a sterilized 2-quart jar.

2   Add the vodka or gin and stir gently. Cover and store in a dark place for 10 days. Stir the mix every other day.

3   Strain the mixture through a cheesecloth or coffee filter, discarding the pulp. Strain a second time, using a fresh filter or a clean cheesecloth. Add the sugar to the juice, stir, and pour the mixture into a sterilized glass bottle. Store in a dark place for 4 weeks. Use within 1 year.

*Yield:*   36 ounces

# Healthy Seed Treats

*Remember those salted pumpkin seed treats you enjoyed as a kid? Now you can make your own, courtesy of your microwave oven and care-package them up for little gifts for kids away at summer camp and college. If you've never had them before, try this recipe just for fun. When you carve your Halloween pumpkin, save all the seeds you scoop out—they make delicious treats that are good for you as well as tasty.*

**1/2 cup salt**
**4 cups water**
**2 cups sunflower, pumpkin, melon,**
*or*
**Squash seeds, cleaned**

1   Make a mixture of the salt and water and soak the seeds in the mixture for 12 hours.

2   Dry the seeds in paper toweling and blot off excess moisture. Place dried seeds on a microwave tray in a single layer. Microwave on medium power for 2 minutes and then on low for 6 minutes. Rotate and stir. Continue on low power for 3 more minutes. Cool and store in an airtight container. Seeds will keep well for 4 to 6 weeks.

**Idea:**
*You can salt or season the seeds, depending on your tastes, with **Sesame Salt**, page 145, or another combination of your favorite spices.*

**Yield:**   16 ounces

# Instant Trail Mix

*Wean your kids away from candy with a trail mix that's healthy as well as tasty. Store individual servings of this mixture in plastic sandwich bags and pack one with your child's lunch or in a camper's backpack for a healthy, high-energy alternative to a candy bar. See **Healthy Seed Treats**, page 245, for how to prepare your own seeds for this mixture.*

**1 cup sunflower seeds**
**1 cup almonds**
**1 cup hazelnuts**
**1 cup raisins**
**1/2 cup unsweetened coconut, shredded**
**2 cups various dried fruits:**
**Bananas, pineapple, apricots, apples**

1   Mix all ingredients and microwave on low power for 2 minutes. Check for dryness and microwave on medium power for 1 minute more, if necessary.

2   Store the mixture in an airtight container. Make up individual snack packs in plastic bags and store the individual packs in the airtight container as well. The snack mix will keep for 2 to 4 months on the pantry shelf.

*Yield:*   6 cups

# Chewy Citrus Candies

*These tasty candies are all natural and keep for months without refrigeration. You can use any kind of citrus for this recipe, and a nice variety of peel will give you a good range of color and flavor for your dishes. No matter what citrus you use—orange, lemon, lime, tangerine, grapefruit—remember to scrape away the white pith under the peel, because it tastes bitter.*

**2 cups citrus peel**
**8 1/2 cups water**
**1 cup sugar**

1   Wash and dry fruit carefully before using. Remove peel from fruit with a vegetable peeler or sharp paring knife. Trim all pith away and cut peel into narrow strips about 1 inch long.

2   Place peel in a bowl with 2 cups water and microwave on medium power for 2 minutes and then on low for 3 minutes. Drain, add 2 more cups water and microwave on low for another 3 minutes. Repeat until peel has been simmered and drained 4 times. Set aside to cool.

3   Combine 1 cup sugar and the remaining 1/2 cup water and microwave to a boil on high power for 3 minutes until sugar dissolves. Add the drained peel. Microwave on medium power for 2 minutes and continue on low until peel has absorbed the liquid (about 5 more minutes).

4   Spread peel on a rack to dry. Roll the candied peel in sugar and continue to air-dry on wax paper or plastic for 24 hours. Store in an airtight container. Candied peel will keep for 2 to 4 months on the pantry shelf.

*Yield:*   16 ounces

# Almond Treats

*Sugared almond candies were always a favorite of mine when I was younger. Now you can treat your kids to the same sweet little nuggets without having to run to the candy store when you run out. A jar of these snacking treats can also be a welcome gift to someone who can use a little comforting. If you prefer, other nuts, such as filberts or macadamia nuts, can be substituted for the almonds.*

**1 cup sugar**
**1 cup honey**
**1/2 cup water**
**1 pound unblanched whole almonds**
**1 teaspoon cinnamon**
**1 teaspoon allspice**

1    Dissolve the sugar in water by microwaving on high power for 3 minutes. Add honey and microwave on high power for 2 more minutes, or until mixture is thick.

2    Add nuts and microwave on medium until the nuts start to crackle, about 4 minutes. Sprinkle on the cinnamon and allspice, stir and microwave on low power for 2 minutes more, or until mixture is dry.

*Yield:* 1 pound

# Sugared Pecans

**1/3 cup butter or margarine**
**1/4 cup sugar**
**1/2 teaspoon cinnamon**
**1/4 teaspoon ground ginger**
**1 pound pecan halves**

1   Microwave butter, sugar, and spices in a bowl on medium power for 3 minutes, or until butter melts completely. Pour mixture over the pecans, making sure to coat all the nuts.

2   Microwave in a shallow tray for 6 minutes on medium power. Stir and continue on medium for 2 more minutes. Cool and store in an airtight container. Nuts will keep well for 4 to 6 weeks.

*Yield:*  1 pound

# Fruit Nut Balls

*Let a child have a hand, literally, with this recipe. It's fun to mix everything up, and the children can get a whole new appreciation of "candy" if they make up some of their own.*

**2/3 cup sweetened condensed milk**
**2 teaspoons vanilla extract**
**1/4 cup nuts, finely chopped**
**1/3 cup unsweetened coconut, shredded**
**1/3 cup raisins**
**1/2 cup dried fruit**
**1/2 cup instant-style rolled oats**

1   Mix all ingredients together and let the mixture sit for 30 minutes before forming into balls.

2   Butter your hands and shape the mixture into small balls. Microwave at low/medium power on a flat microwave dish for 4 to 5 minutes.

3   Remove from pan before candy is completely cool and place the balls on a wire rack. Cool before storing in a tightly closed container. The candy will keep for 2 to 4 weeks.

*Yield:*  13 ounces

# Peach Chutney

*Chutney stimulates the appetite and cuts the heavy taste of most meats. Sweet chutney is especially easy on the palate during the summer. This recipe makes a nice batch of chutney that you can use to accompany main courses or serve as a before-dinner palate teaser with some crackers or toasted wheat bread.*

**8 pounds peaches**
**5 cups white vinegar**
**1/2 cup onion, chopped**
**1/2 cup sugar**
**1/2 cup raisins**
**1/4 cup mustard seeds**
**2 ounces fresh gingerroot, minced**
*or*
**1 teaspoon ground ginger**
**2 tablespoons red pepper**
**5 to 6 cloves garlic, chopped**

1   Peel, pit, and quarter the peaches. Place peaches in a bowl and add 2 cups of the vinegar. Microwave on medium power for 6 minutes, or until peaches are soft.

2   Add the remaining 3 cups of vinegar and the rest of the ingredients. Microwave on medium power for 5 minutes more.

3   Pour mixture, while still hot, into sterilized canning jars and store in the refrigerator. Chutney will keep for 2 to 4 months while refrigerated.

*Yield:* 48 ounces

# East India Chutney

**12 apples**
**4 cups brown sugar**
**8 cups apple cider**
**4 cups raisins**
**1/4 cup dry mustard**
**1/4 cup ground ginger**
**1 tablespoon salt**

1   Core and chop apples, combine all ingredients, and place 2 cups of the mixture in a glass microwave bowl. Bring to a boil by microwaving on high power for 5 minutes. Check and stir mixture, return to microwave, and cook at high power for 2 minutes and then at medium power for 10 minutes. Apples should be thoroughly cooked. Repeat procedure, in 2-cup batches, until all of the mixture has been cooked.

2   Pour mixture, while still hot, into sterilized canning jars and store in the refrigerator. Chutney will keep for 2 to 4 months while refrigerated.

*Yield:*  48 ounces

# New Year's Brandied Peaches

*This recipe should be made well in advance of holiday or gift-giving time. Since peaches are plentiful in late summer, you will want to take advantage of their low prices then and make up your jars, but because the flavors must mellow and stew awhile, you will have to wait until Christmas or the New Year to enjoy this treat.*

**2 pounds peaches**
**2 cups sugar**
**2 cups water**
**Brandy**

1   Peel, halve, and pit peaches.

2   Microwave the sugar and water in a glass bowl on high power for 3 minutes to dissolve the sugar. Add the peaches, and microwave on medium power for 5 minutes.

3   Pour off the syrup into a measuring cup and combine with an equal quantity of brandy.

4   Pack peaches in sterilized wide-mouth glass jars without crowding them too tightly. Pour the syrup-brandy mixture over the peaches to cover. Close the jars tightly and put them away on a cool, dark pantry shelf to rest for 6 months.

***Ideas:***
*Pour peaches over vanilla ice cream, adding a dollop of sweetened whipped cream. Save every bit of the liquid from your peaches and you can add more fruit throughout the year, indefinitely.*

***Yield:***  32 ounces

# 10

# Sensational and Snappy Gift Baskets

*The following suggestions for gift baskets make clever use of the recipes from **Zapcrafts**. You can purchase inexpensive baskets and paint and decorate them in a style appropriate to the type of gift you are giving—try pretty pastels for a baby, dried flowers and ribbons for a woman, or tiny toys and candies for a child. You can also use containers other than baskets, of course, such as painted tins, small wooden boxes—almost anything that will hold a few surprises or treasures. Ideas for types of containers, as well as suggested contents, are also given here.*

# *Instructions*

# Christmas Alone Cheer-Me-Up

*If you know that someone you love will be spending Christmas alone, try gathering a basketful of goodies, each wrapped separately, with instructions to open one gift each day. Such a thoughtful gesture will let the distant loved one know that you are thinking about him or her all through the holiday season.*

## Container Suggestions

*Try using one of a pair of festive holiday-colored woolen stockings or socks. Roll up the mate and tuck it into the sock, and you will have another gift.*

*Or, send a big Christmas piñata (page 106) that you or your children have constructed, and fill it to the brim with goodies.*

## Items to Include

**A paperback book**
**A favorite album**

## Recipes

**Spicy Pomander Balls (page 208)**
**New Year's Brandied Peaches (page 252)**
**Cranberry Liqueur (page 203)**
**A selection of Herb Teas (page 153)**
**Microwave Potpourri (page 98)**

# Bridal Shower Basket

*A particularly treasured gift I received at my bridal shower was a big laundry basket filled with all the little things you always forget about but really must have to set up your new home—the measuring spoons and wire whisks and clothes-pins and sponges—nothing very glamorous, but everything that is necessary and welcome when you need it most. It's also fun to send along some items to make the wedding night extra special.*

## Container Suggestions

*A wicker laundry basket or pretty clothing hamper would be very appreciated, but think about special, one-of-a-kind containers for the Pear Cordial and Soft Soap, since you've gone to all the trouble to make the items yourself.*

## Items to Include

A copy of *Zapcrafts*
Measuring cups and spoons
2 cordial glasses
2 matching mugs

## Recipes

St. Valentine's Pear Cordial (page 240)
Microwave Potpourri (page 98)
Midnight Popcorn Munchies (page 177)
Instant Mulling Mix (page 207)
Rum Coffee (page 206)
Scented Soft Soap (page 55)

# Summer Camp Send-off

*Do you have a camper in your family, especially a first-time camper who may experience a bit of homesickness? Send along his or her first "care package" with favorite snacks, lots of stationery, and "trade 'em offs," handy little items your camper can trade with bunkmates and other campers. Hint:* **Caramel Ninja Turtles** *have been through four campers and are the best trade 'em offs there are.*

## Container Suggestion

*A box that the camper can hide private treasures in, lock up, and slide under a bunk will be most appreciated. Make sure you include a lock and key if the child is not old enough to remember a combination, and keep an extra copy of the key at home.*

## Items to Include

**A supply of stamped, home-addressed envelopes**
**Pretty or snazzy letter paper**

## Recipes

**Instant Trail Mix (page 246)**
**Chewie Fruit (page 142)**
**Individually wrapped S'mores (page 183)**
**Caramel Ninja Turtles (page 180)**
**Instant Hot Cocoa (page 167)**
**Midnight Popcorn Munchies (page 177)**
**Sparkling Saturday Cereal (page 166)**

# Bon Voyage Basket

*When friends or family plan a trip, they don't always think about the comforting last-minute little things that can make their time away from home special, especially if they're going to be on vacation for an extended period. Here is a collection of ideas for travelers, friends, or family going on that once-in-a lifetime cruise or second honeymoon.*

## Container Suggestion

*A small carry-on-size piece of soft luggage that can be folded and packed for coming home would be appreciated.*

## Items to Include

**A travel game set for the plane trip:
checkers, backgammon, chess, or playing cards
A few dollars' worth of currency
for the destination country
(to spend on cab fare, drinks, emergencies)
A paperback book or novel
A blank journal
Film and developing-service envelopes
Stamped and home-addressed envelopes**

## Recipes

**Deep Tanning Oil (page 42)
Rose Beads (page 219)
Almond Treats (page 248)
Jiffy Insect Repellent (page 74)
Vitamin E Aftershave (page 27)
Athlete's Friction Bath (page 56)
Scented Soft Soap (page 55)**

# New Apartment
# or
# First House Warming

*In the rush of closing, packing, moving, and unpacking, new homeowners or apartment renters will inevitably overlook one or more of the last-minute items that can make the first night in a new place an adventure or a less-than-perfect experience. Why don't you do some of the thinking your friends will forget to do and send them a housewarming starter basket?*

## Container Suggestions

*The last thing a new apartment needs is another bag or box to unpack, so wrap your gifts up in a laundry bag or a big wicker plant holder.*

## Items to Include

**Paper plates and cups**
**Plastic silverware**

## Recipes

**Herbal Air Spray for the At-Home Spa (page 59)**
**Spicy Pomander Balls (page 208)**
**Microwave Potpourri (page 98)**
**Moth-Scat Mixture (page 100)**
**Soft Soaps (page 54)**
**Homemade Bagel Chips (page 134)**
**Snacker Jacks (page 175)**

# Happy Retirement Goodie Box

*Retirement can be a mixed blessing. On the one hand, the retiree can step away from the daily grind of keeping to a relentless daily schedule; on the other hand, the sudden shift from responsibility to leisure can be unnerving. Show your parent or friend that you care with a thoughtful gift basket that will help ease the transition.*

## Container Suggestion

*If the retired person is determined to stay in good shape and live forever, help out by selecting a first-rate knapsack that will encourage endless, wonderful walks and ramrod-straight, teenage-young posture.*

## Items to Include

**Magazine subscriptions**
**Tools, paints, hobby items**

## Recipes

**Sea Salt Seasoning (page 76)**
**Chapped Skin Miracle Solution (page 75)**
**Forever Young Facial Cream (page 5)**
**Good Digestion Tea (page 77)**
**Swedish Spa Bath for Charley Horse (71)**
**Coffee Liqueur (page 238)**
**Sweet Berry Cordial  (page 242)**
**Gourd Bird Feeder and Nest (page 116)**

# Men's Good Grooming Kit

*Give the man on your gift list a basket full of some of your own personalized items made with love. Most of these pampering treats and nibbles are exactly the kind of thing most men never think to buy for themselves.*

## Container Suggestions

*A good leather dop kit is always appreciated; most men seem to gnaw and abuse the ones they carry on trips. If your gift recipient is an executive, a cloth attaché case is a welcome change from the standard boxy leather ones, and it's just as rugged.*

## Items to Include

**A subscription to the Wall Street Journal**
**A manicure set with instructions**

## Recipes

**Glasnost Hot Vodka Rubdown (page 50)**
**Athlete's Friction Bath (page 56)**
**Cucumber Aftershave Splash (page 26)**
**Euro-spa Hair Restorative (page 39)**
**Deep Tanning Oil (page 42)**
**Healthy Seed Treats (page 245)**

# Gourmet's Delight

*A bottle of fine vintage wine is always welcome. If you are not sure of your wine selecting ability and want to leave the choosing to the wine store salesman, remember to specify exactly how much you wish to spend.*

*In your best penmanship, write out a favorite recipe or two that you have enjoyed making and include it in the gift.*

## Container Suggestion

*An earthenware cooking container or antique soup tureen.*

## Items to Include

**Any new and interesting kitchen gadget
Raw ingredients from your garden:
tomatoes, berries, even zucchini in season**

## Recipes

**St. Valentine's Pear Cordial (page 240)
Tam o' Shanter's Butterscotch (page 228)
Hot Peppery Mustard (page 234)
Sugared Pecans (page 248)
Microwave Oven Freshener (page 223)
Sweet Berry Syrups (page 231)
Peach Orange Sauce (page 197)
Quick Sugar Flowers (page 189)
East India Chutney (page 251)**

# Additional Basket Ideas

*The practice of collecting a basketful of good cheer to suit any occasion is an easy habit to get into. Once you get started, you will find it hard to stop thinking of interesting, handy, fancy, or just plain fun items to tuck into a special container. Following are some ideas for themes or impromptu occastions for clever gifts.*

**Pet Pampers Hampers**
**Children's Play Box**
**Roughing-It-in-the-Woods Knapsack**
**Herb Basket**
**Summer Bounty Basket**
**Wine Basket**
**Women's Bath Basket**
**Car Care Basket**
**Gardener's Basket**
**Arts and Crafts Basket**
**Grandparents-Are-Nice Basket**
**Congratulations to the Proud Parents (or Grandparents)**
**Mother-to-Mother Basket**
**Get-Well Basket**
**Picnic in the Park for Two**
**Baby Shower Basket**
**College Care Basket**
**Child's Birthday Basket**
**Bread 'n Butter Thank You Basket**

# Index

# Q-R